WALKING TH
OF THE MI.

Volume One

by

Michael R. Kettle

Walking the Canals of the Midlands

copyright © Michael R. Kettle 1999
reprint 1999

ISBN 0 907 616 47 X

Published in Great Britain by

Able Publishing
13 Station Road
Knebworth
Herts. SG3 6AP

Tel: (01438) 812320/814316
Fax: (01438) 815232
Email: able@dial.pipex.com
Web site: http://www.ablepublishing.co.uk

COMMON COMFREY

This book is dedicated to British Waterways, The Inland Waterways Association, and the many groups, and individuals, who have given their time to the restoration, and maintenance of all British Canals.

My thanks also go to anyone with whom I have talked, about the project, for their suggestions, ideas, and support. Without that assistance, this book would not have appeared.

Back cover illustration and nature drawings by S. Woodward.

All photographs by the Author

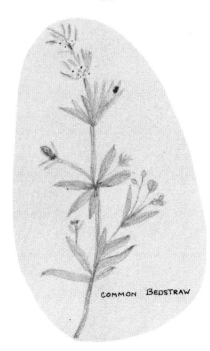

COMMON BEDSTRAW

MEADOW CRANESBILL

TEASEL

CONTENTS

All distances are approximate.

Introduction

I suppose it would be true to say that I first walked along canals at the tender age of five years. However, that experience was limited to accompanying a Police War Reservist along the 'Sling', a small section of the Staffs/Worcs, which runs through part of industrial Kidderminster. This walking relieved the boredom of a small child during school holidays, and took me out from under the feet of a Mother who was trying to run the family business, whilst Dad served in a wartime job at the nearby British Sugar factory.

My interest was held by laden barges, being towed at leisurely pace by heavy horses. I have since learned that these carried coal, and other freight between Stourport, the Black Country, and further afield, by means of the various waterways. Where towpaths changed sides, the horses sometimes needed to be unhitched from the boat, to be connected once more beyond the obstacle. Some bridges, however were designed with a complete split down the centre, thus making it unnecessary to untie the horse. Where ropes came into contact with metal or brickwork, the years of friction caused grooving. These marks are readily visible at many places years onward.

This experience may have begun my interest in canals, but for some fifteen years, I have seriously walked along various ones, read as many books as possible on the subject, and the result is this book.

Most canals were built during a period of the latter half of the Eighteenth Century, by famous names, such as James Brindley and Thomas Telford. They were made necessary by the poor quality of the cart tracks, which served as roads, and the requirement of the larger manufacturers to send finished items to the various ports. There was also a great need to obtain raw materials more swiftly. The coming of the Industrial Revolution, heightened this need, so until the arrival of railways, the canal often provided the only means of bulk transportation.

After the invention of the steam engine, the canals had more and more competition, until, by the 1920's, their use had greatly declined, and only the pressures of the second world war, briefly revived the need for such slow transport.

Fortunately for the people of the 1990's, the disuse of many waterways was halted, then reversed by far-seeing individuals, who realised that we could not afford to lose this great heritage.

Now, we regard the canals as places for holidays, and recreational travel, and they offer much pleasure to both walkers, and boaters alike.

The various stretches of canal differ from each other. Apart from the different designers and their methods, the geographical lie of the ground has made it necessary to provide more locks, where a larger gradient requires them. As an example, in a four mile stretch of the Worcester & Birmingham, there are thirty locks, whilst in a similar length on the Staffs/Worcs, there are only four.

Some parts give the impression of never having been put to use by industry, whilst others are unable to deny their history. Each one has it's own characteristics, and was designed to adapt to the terrain.

Narrow boat people had to be a tough breed, often called 'Water Gypsies' a derogatory term, but they knew little of the life of a town dweller.

Lock-keepers were everywhere in evidence, until the lack of freight made them redundant. They have largely been replaced by holiday crews.

This book is intended to encourage as many as possible to enjoy the many quiet and easy walks through the beautiful countryside, and to be aware of the History, Natural History, and Geography of the area through which they are passing.

This was written through several years, and in all seasons, but the basic information remains the same.

Michael R. Kettle 1999.

Part One

The Birmingham to Worcester Canal

Section 1   Hopwood - Tardebigge

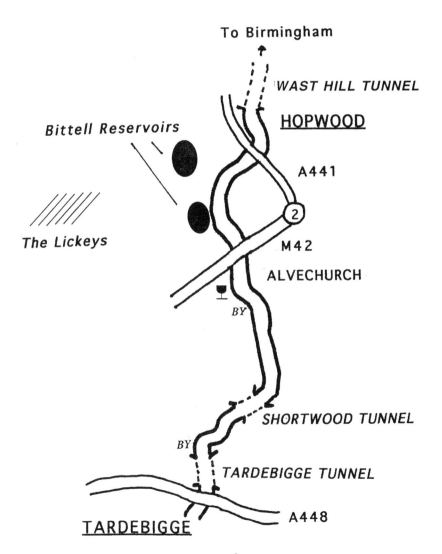

To Birmingham

WAST HILL TUNNEL

HOPWOOD

Bittell Reservoirs

A441

The Lickeys

M42

ALVECHURCH

BY

SHORTWOOD TUNNEL

BY

TARDEBIGGE TUNNEL

A448

TARDEBIGGE

An act of Parliament, dated 1791, enabled the construction of this canal to begin, however, it was not completed until 1815, due to various financial problems. The total cost was in the region of £400,000, for the 29 mile waterway, which illustrates one of the problems in raising funds, when comparing this figure with the £100,000 for the Staffordshire and Worcestershire Canal. Lengthwise, there was not a great deal of difference, if anything the Worcester & Birmingham is a mile or two shorter.

Credit for the original survey work, is attributed to one Josiah Clowes, although Thomas Telford, and others, may have given the benefit of their experience from elsewhere.

In deciding where to commence a walk along this canal, the obvious point would be the junction with the Stratford on Avon Canal, at Kings Norton. However, the lengthy Wast Hill Tunnel, make it more practical to begin at Hopwood, just beyond the Birmingham City boundary. For those using their own transport to reach that point, there are limited parking places nearby, though the most obvious one, at Hopwood House, means the courtesy of asking permission from the landlord before so doing. There are however good public transport connections, either by Midland Red services, or by British Rail, to either Alvechurch, or Barnt Green stations.

Hopwood, still a quiet village, on the fringe of the larger conurbation, would be the last to claim that there is much of interest there. However, it is situated on a lock-free stretch of waterway, which means level walking, and it is clean and tidy.

We descend to the towpath by means of a gently sloping lane, and the early part is a peaceful, tree lined, wide stretch of water. Over to the right, behind the trees, is a lane which connects Hopwood with Barnt Green, via the side of Bittell reservoir. Then the route turns away from the lane, and surrounding farmland, heading for the reservoir, a short distance away. As we approach the dyke, which takes the canal along one side of the reservoir, look out for the bright building over the far side, which was once the property occupied by the Water Bailiff, but is now just a tasteful reminder of former days. Along the dyke, the canal is straight. Private, local craft are moored there, with a superb view across the open water. In Spring, and Autumn, Bewick Swans often use the lake (for that is how it appears), for resting and feeding, on their way between Siberia and Slimbridge wild fowl trust, or vice-versa. Mute Swans, and other species of water bird can also be seen, and so binoculars are a useful item for the walker.

We leave the reservoir, pass under a humped bridge, then over a blue-bricked flat bridge at Aqueduct Lane, and already we are getting near to Alvechurch. Now quietened by the construction of a link road, and the M42, this was once a very busy point on the Birmingham to Redditch main highway. Now, the traffic is scarcely noticeable from the noise angle. If anyone is using an old map, the next section will now provide a puzzle, for during the construction of the M42 Motorway, during 1984-1985, the canal was diverted. A new section, almost a quarter of a mile in length, was created, turning right under the new bridge, and away from the original course. The old waterway was blocked at one end, to create a backwater, which is now popular with anglers, and a new brick and wood bridge constructed to link the new towpath, with the old path on the far side of what remains of the original canal. The new part is very wide, has a large curve, and was very carefully done, so that the area was not spoiled by the necessary alteration.

I was lucky enough to be walking this new section on March 9th 1985, when the official opening took place. Despite inclement weather in the winter months, the whole changeover took a mere five months, quite an achievement.

We have now crossed to the original waterway, and it curves to the right, to run along the top edge of the town, parallel with the single track railway (now electrified) which runs to Redditch only. The towpath offers views at roof-top level, and is a popular walk for locals. Several rear gardens have access to the path, which now snakes its way under the railway, and a second bridge, carrying a side road into the country. There are the remains of some former industrial premises on the far side, also The Crown public house, which would be especially welcome to anyone who has walked the route the opposite way.

Very shortly, the waterway loops to the right, past one or two permanent moorings, and we see a variety of narrow boats as we pass under an arched bridge. This is the Alvechurch Boat Centre, which is very busy during the season. My impression is, that this is one of, if not the, best laid out, and kept marina on this canal. It is usually busy, but does not spoil the peaceful countryside. Just past this point, there is a black and white period residence, but no reference to this is on my map, so I do not know the name of it.

After once more turning left, the waterway narrows considerably, where it passes over a small stream. As we approached, a Green Woodpecker flew over the water, breath-taking in it's red and green plumage. It was long gone, before the camera could be focused, but no illustration in bird books seems to do it justice.

Further turns, and a humped bridge is reached at Cobley Hill. Few motorists dare pass over without a hooted warning, for the road here is completely masked by the severity of the hump. Once under the low brickwork, the canal becomes open and wide, and the views are of open Worcestershire. To the East is the village of Rowney Green, then beyond can be seen the commencement of Redditch new town.

Woods reach toward the West bank, and in a few yards, others are close to the East bank. Ahead of us, there is a tunnel entrance, with the towpath climbing steeply away from the water. This is Shortwood, a tunnel 562 metres in length, with no pathway through. We follow the old horse path to the hill, just as horses would have climbed after being unhitched. In pre-mechanical times, the boats were propelled through tunnels by "legging", crew members lying flat on their backs over planks, across the boat, 'walking' along the walls. At the far end, the ropes were once more attached to the animal where it remained until either the next tunnel, or the next time the towpath changed sides.

We follow the path through the wood, which swings Westward over the tunnel, then turns Southward through a field. At the far side, we have to search for the resumption of the pathway, and for a while, there is no sign of the water, and I think my sense of direction has let me down. Once over a stile, however, and we reach a deep cutting lined with trees on both sides, and the pathway descends to the canal.

On looking back through the darkness, daylight shows clearly, and we consider it to be a short tunnel. I doubt if the "leggers" would have agreed. Certainly, we walked far more than 562 metres with the necessary detour.

The countryside opens out, with the Eastern bank (now the far side), sloping down towards Hewell Grange. Once the home of the Earls of Plymouth, this house is now a remand home and prison. We can now see the tower of Tardebigge church, at least the top of it, but there is still a little way to walk.

We pass under an old farm bridge, at which point, the towpath narrows, and with more vegetation, the next few yards are a little difficult. Not many people walk this stretch, but we are some way from any sizeable habitation. The waterway turns nearly ninety degrees, and there are boats moored just ahead. Very soon, we need to leave the towpath again and use lanes to bypass Tardebigge tunnel.

To those with a need to return to Hopwood, now would seem to be the right moment, but for those using public transport, a bus route passes Tardebigge itself, and Bromsgrove Railway station is about two miles along the road.

Bailiffs' House - Bittell

Section 2 Tardebigge to Stoke Prior 4³/₄ miles

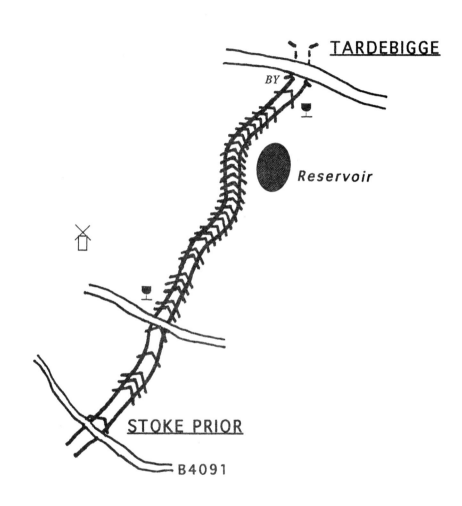

TARDEBIGGE

BY

Reservoir

STOKE PRIOR

B4091

Tardebigge wharf is situated at the head of a long flight of locks. On this walk, one will pass, and possibly repass, thirty. In some cases there is a small gap between flights, but often there are several close together. This section is a very comfortable stroll, taking up to two hours, depending on what items of interest one sees on the way.

On leaving the main road, and the tunnel exit, just over the right shoulder, the pathway slopes gently down to the canal side. The wharf itself, is quite busy on weekdays, but nowhere near as bustling as in the heyday of the waterway. A few boats are moored across the water, some appear to be residential, and some are in the throes of repair.

The Top Lock, is number 58, and is some twenty feet deep. Originally, this was a mechanical lift, not a lock. This is quite deep by most standards on the Worcester & Birmingham, and extra care is needed when negotiating such a lock. Close by, stands a large, renovated cottage, with information about the canal, in a case near the towpath. From here, it is a short step to bridge no 56, just an ordinary farm track crossing.

To the left, on top of the hill, stands Tardebigge Church, giving the walker a chance to see it's unique tower. Just below the top spire, there are spaces right through the structure. For what reason, I know not.

Once again, the path is in excellent state of repair, since being renewed in the recent few years. There are small woods along either side, and we notice that the lower branches, overhanging the water, have a distinctive line of mud, though above the normal waterline. We realise that this is due to the large volume of water released into the section just below the steep lock, which increases depth momentarily after downward passage of craft.

Rounding a corner, we see bridge no 55. No metal plate, but the numbers have been etched in concrete at the centre of the arch. We can now see a group of locks, but just before them is a large building at the towpath's edge. This is a restaurant, displaying the name "Tylers Lock on the Water". Originally, this building was the Engine House, housing machinery to help control water levels in the lock flight. When one realises that the average narrow lock takes about 90,000 gallons of water, to fill, it can be appreciated, that where several locks are close together, it requires a system to replace what has been lost. Replacement water comes from the reservoir nearby.

Locks 57 - 53, are close together, though opposite 53, there is a mechanical sluice to drain excess water into a nearby stream. There are two cottages, in sheltered positions, and through the garden of the lower one, can be seen a large stretch of water. This is the reservoir for these locks, but it is now used by anglers and by a variety of water birds alike. Ducks were much in evidence, but a trio of Great Crested Grebes were busily diving into the depths. Two more locks, 52 and 51 take the path and of course, the canal, below the level of the reservoir. Consequently, the lower end of that water is secured by a massive embankment.

At lock 50, a footbridge (no. 54) leads from the reservoir to a parking area, thence to a lane. Anglers going to fish use this regularly. Somewhere at this section, there was a vivid red, spotted among the seeding weeds, over the water. Closer inspection revealed a black head, also other brilliant plumage. A Bullfinch was busy feeding. As I had not seen one of these colourful birds for many years, the sighting ranked a very close third to Kingfishers and Herons in my list of important species to be seen along our waterways.

Another feature of the water replenishment on canals, is the overflow. Varying from the designer's preference, according to which canal one is walking, the ones on the Birmingham-Worcester, are simple concrete sloping channels, heading down to the next level. As these are not protected by fencing or walls, they are normally placed on the furthest side, away from towpath.

Locks 49 - 45 are grouped close to each other at this point, and a much smaller cottage stands as if to guard them. Another footbridge, no. 52 is here. What happened to 53? We haven't a clue, and there is no sign that there was one. Another mystery.

Locks 44 - 41 take up a few more yards of the walk, also bridge no. 51. Another cottage is close to lock 40, and looking across the open fields beyond, we can see the Malvern Hills, distinguishable by their exclusive shape, certainly known to Worcestershire folk. Yet a further group, 39 - 36, and another bridge, no. 50. All along this stretch, during early September, are trees laden with Elderberries. I christen it

Elderberry Avenue, but many are inaccessible without a ladder, since they are at the foot of a steep embankment, just out of reach of anyone on the towpath. Probably why they are still on the trees!

There is a modern property with a large parcel of ground. Does not appear to have been converted from a lock-keepers cottage, it is a little too far from the canal side.

Three more locks, no's. 33 - 31, another cottage, definitely an original, and bridge no. 49. This is covered with creeper.

When we reach lock 30, it appears that we may have come to the end of the flight. We are on fairly level ground, surrounded by fields full of Cattle, Donkeys and Sheep. Also a large development of Barn conversions stands just beyond the animals.

Just to contradict our thoughts, lock 29 is just around the next left hand turn, but that really is the last of the main "Tardebigge" flight.

Watching the various boats negotiate locks is fascinating. Some crews have the process down to a fine art, whilst others struggle to cope. Methods vary, according to the number of persons on board, and with other craft in the same section. With larger crews, some members go ahead to prepare the water level in the next lock, by means of paddles and gates, often before their boat has left the previous lock. Those remaining on board return the lock they have just left,. to readiness for the next boat. Where there are only small crews, the process takes longer, whilst waiting to reach the next obstacle before preparation. When there are other craft, especially if they are travelling in the opposite direction, common sense, and courtesy demands that, alternate turns of up or down are exercised.

All of this is time consuming, thus crews need to be aware of the time involved, in order to calculate their daily mileage, and so ensure that they reach the boatyard on time, at the end of their holiday.

The scenery is now totally rural, only farms and cottages in sight of the pathway. Our route now runs parallel to the railway, passing down the Lickey incline south westerly toward Gloucester and beyond. So far, the trains can be heard, but not seen, but we are aware that it is a very busy line. Strange to think that the railways came very close to closing the canals altogether, yet now, each has it's place in our society, only the cost of both has become restrictive.

17

Across the fields to the West, we see the spire of St John's Church, Bromsgrove, also rooftops of the town itself. Once just a small market town, now a large conurbation with many new estates, as with many Worcestershire centres.

A Magpie chatters in the Hawthorn, but not many hedgerow birds at that moment. A temporary absence, I suspect.

Cattle graze quietly nearby, but there are not so many in the late 1990's than a decade before, due to the harsh Euro regulations. Now, we can clearly see the masts at Wychbold, which will remain in view for some miles yet. Butterflies are in abundance on a warm summer's day. Many small tortoiseshell, but some meadow browns, painted ladies, peacocks, a few common blues, and the ubiquitous large whites. I cannot help but wonder why we seldom see red admirals as in my younger days.

We look up and think we are in Holland. There a few hundred yards to the West, on top of a hill, is a Windmill. This is the restored, and working Mill at the Avoncroft Museum, just South of Bromsgrove, at the heart of a popular and educational site of restored buildings. It can be clearly seen from three sides, and for anyone who may not have already been there, well worth a visit. The most convenient walk to this centre, is a few locks further down, and over the bridge near the Queens Head.

Each turn, brings more locks into view. The boat crews will most likely think "not more", but to the walker, a delight to the eye, for such items add interest to the exercise.

We have passed under many bridges, carrying lanes or cart tracks but the towpath continues on the same side of the water, the only descents being the steep paths by the side of locks.

Water is a wonderful, yet powerful element. Often it has a very distinctive smell, it also produces a variety of sound, as it flows through locks and paddles. At one moment, it is as if gentle music were playing, at another, there is a roar as if a powerful engine was operating. The variation in colour offers the painter a choice from muddy brown, after the passage of craft, to a reflective blue from the sky with a myriad hues in between. When the water is still, the reflections are quite spectacular.

There has been some refurbishment of locks, and bridges. New gates have replaced the originals in many cases, but some brickwork seems like original workmanship.

We are asked if there are many more locks to traverse, although most crews have maps which provide that information. However, the most asked question is "how far to the next place for a drink?". When human beings are relaxed, in holiday mood, they communicate readily with others on the waterway. Certainly the vast majority wave cheerily, and pass the time of day. I like to discover where the crews come from, and am surprised at the large number from overseas. Such conversations are pleasant diversions, especially if legs are becoming tired from lengthy walking.

The railway sounds closer, in fact as we reach lock 33, the two forms of travel converge, and for a while, we can see the various trains. It is only momentary, for we are soon once again in the world of leisurely travel, and the accompanying peace.

Now, that peace is interrupted by the sound of low-flying aircraft. Several Hercules transports, pass overhead, a mere hundred or so feet over the canal. Vortices of moisture can be seen over the wing surfaces, especially if there is some cloud cover. Now they head in the direction of the Severn Valley, their four great engines clawing at the air, in a display of power. Once more, the ancient and the modern have come together, and for someone who also enjoys the sight of aircraft, an added interest to the walk.

At last, we are clear of the main flight of locks, and as the next corner is rounded, a long straight stretch leads to the Queens Head on the far side. This modernised, and enlarged hostelry has moorings for several boats, but is mostly renowned for generous Carvery meals patronised by locals, and by people from further afield.

Access is gained by crossing the bridge, into the Car Park, and in through the original building.

On a warm day, it also provides smaller meals, and a variety of liquid refreshment for walkers. I certainly appreciated the rest a visit afforded.

Resuming the walk, we are now on one of the flattest sections of this canal. There are open fields on both sides, and Horses and Cattle are much in evidence. Here, we have Swallows, in Summer, wheeling back and forth over the water, in endless flight. The farms seem more modern and mechanised, and there are luxurious properties in the hamlets.

Boat crews, after their long descent through the flight, are now able to relax, and enjoy an almost lock free journey, for a while. Our walk from Tardebigge has taken a little over ninety minutes, but the average for narrow boats have probably taken between two and three hours to cover the same stretch.

Once under the next bridge, the character of the waterway changes. We are now in a shaded, tree lined section, leading to Stoke Prior. There are many moorings, some for privately owned boats, but also for the coming Boatyard. This is Black Prince, a holiday hire centre, from which many crews commence their cruise. From here, it is a short step to the Navigation public house, another popular eating place. On the far side of the bridge from the 'Navvy' the road passes, firstly a new trading estate, then the renowned Harris Brush works, from whence many of our decorating paint brushes emanate. We have the first signs of serious industry since our walk began, and this is now the point to either retrace ones steps to Tardebigge, or alternatively, to seek public transport to either Bromsgrove, or Droitwich. However, one should be advised that here, the public transport is rather intermittent.

Stoke Wharf

Section 3 Stoke Prior to Hanbury Wharf 4 miles

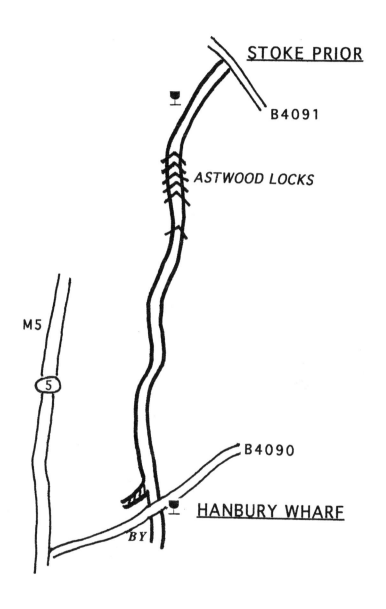

STOKE PRIOR

B4091

ASTWOOD LOCKS

M5

5

B4090

HANBURY WHARF

BY

After passing under the road bridge at Stoke Prior, the scene changes to a more industrial one. There is much evidence of previous, and present manufacturing, and to those unprepared for the alteration, it might be rather daunting. However, it should be remembered that canals were built to serve industry, and the miles of countryside and rural landscapes, are a superb bonus.

The path is narrower, and shows signs of fewer walkers using this section, but this very soon changes. Bridges now carry roads into factories, or pipe lines from one site to another. We are again close to the railway, and there are lines branching from the main one, into the manufacturing areas, also in the opposite direction toward Droitwich. Only local knowledge supports this information, and apart from hearing and seeing trains, the walker is not unduly taken from the general solitude of the task in hand.

The first bridge crossing the waterway carries pipes, within an iron framework. It bears the date 1861, and so follows the original canal by fifty years. To the left, the depressions of the late part of the twentieth century can be clearly seen by the derelict buildings, and due to the spaces where factories once stood. The towpath rises where a former water access to premises allowed laden barges to pass in and out. Rope grooves in the masonry can clearly be seen, reminding us, if it were needed, that even up to the early 1950's, horses were quite regularly used to haul barges. On the opposite side, stands a large warehouse complex, where modern transport, in the shape of Juggernauts, has changed carrying habits. The original wall stands firm, preventing drivers from falling into the water whilst trying to negotiate round parked vehicles.

At Stoke Works, which is really a continuation of Stoke Prior, a modern bridge carries a wide road. Despite it's size, the road is not shown on the map as even a 'B' class, but it is obviously well used.

On the far side of the Waterway stand several cottages, also the 'Boat and Railway' public house. This is the meeting place of a branch of the Worcester & Birmingham Canal Society, a body of people whose thoughts and activities greatly help the users of this waterway. We can see that a road runs parallel to the canal, behind those buildings, after which, a school and modern houses create an impression of a larger community, than is the case. As a measure of our progress down the water, we now see the Radio masts at Wychbold close by. Very soon, we reach bridge no. 41. It is humped, and traffic crosses with caution.

Industry and Commerce, have been left behind. Once more we are in deepest rural Worcestershire, and the panorama opens out before our eyes. There are open fields, farms, often surrounded with trees, and Crows, Rooks, and many smaller birds, are much in evidence, carrying out their daily routine.

After a break from locks, we now round a corner to find three, more or less together. The gates have been replaced in recent years, as with many of the locks, so water loss is minimal.

On both sides of the waterway, church towers can be seen across farmland. Wychbold to the West, Hanbury to the East, each of varying design, although they are too far away to really appreciate their origin or size. A new sound intrudes onto the scene. The buzz of traffic from the M5 Motorway can be heard, but the road cannot yet be seen.

We can also hear trains again, and the canal and railway have become closer and run parallel. Locks no. 20, 19 and 18 are now passed. Just beyond no. 18, there is a cream coloured lock cottage where we see that a large garden; together with Hens, Ducks and Geese are all on the far side of the water, reached by the handy bridge. Along the towpath, there is a washing line and we wonder how passers-by fare on washing days. It is now seen that the overflows by these lower locks are smaller, and even more simple constructions. There does not seem to be much risk of flooding, on this section.

The canal, which had been quite wide, narrows through some brick foundations, thus giving rise to the possibility that a bridge had been removed at this point.

The towpath is very well flattened, which, together with a small Car Park over the far side, suggests a popular Angling site. At the edge of the far bank, metal pilings have been installed, as in several previous places. This modern method of repair, is very effective, and despite it's modern appearance, soon blends with the surroundings, especially as vegetation very swiftly covers the work of British Waterways staff. A well kept Hawthorn hedge, on the East side, helps shield the canal from cold winds in winter. The waterway has been continually winding, in various directions, but from lock 17, we have a good quarter of a mile of straight water. However, at the end of that unusual direct route, the waterway swings toward the railway. Over the next bridge, cattle cross and recross and the farm from which they come, is just a short distance away. Now the canal and railway are on a 'collision' course, and it will not be long before they change places.

When I first walked this section of the canal, some fourteen years earlier, I found that the towpath was in very poor condition. Large sections were missing, and the erosion made walking very difficult. Therefore, I was delighted to find, on recent walks, that repairs had been effected, and that walking here is now as pleasant as the remainder of the canal.

The water is well above the level of the surrounding fields, and replacement of the banks had obviously become a vital task. Reeds already cover the metal edges, and in fact grow thickly nearby. In fact the water is quite narrow as a result.

Wildlife is very much in evidence. Rabbits play on the path until disturbed, there seems to be some evidence of Badgers, by the large holes in banks at the edge of the fields, Ducks and Moorhens criss-cross the water, and in the hedges are Wrens, Yellowhammers and Finches.

As already noted, the railway now runs along the East side, and in the far distance, to the West, the Motorway can just be recognised. Since Stoke Prior, there have been fewer cruising boats, but their numbers vary according to the day of the week, and whether or not they are returning to local boatyards.

Around the next corner, we can see the double bridge, which crosses both the main waterway, and the entrance to the Droitwich branch canal. Originally, that waterway linked the Birmingham - Worcester with the river Severn at Hawford, some five miles away on the far side of the town. It was used largely for the carriage of Coal to, and Salt from, the local workings, but fell victim to decay and disuse. Volunteers are gradually restoring this fine example of a Brindley waterway, but lack of funds, and the severity of the task is making it into a very long job indeed.

Where the main road passes over the main canal, there is a sloping path up to the Eagle and Sun. They specialise in Home cooked food, and have the usual refreshments available as well. Judging by the number of cars in their park at meal times, it is well worth the visit. It should also be mentioned that the exterior of this pub is beautifully decorated with seasonal flowers.

Once more, the walker now has a choice of:

1. Returning to StokePrior
2. Walking another section
or 3. Walking a mile or so into Droitwich, for either Bus or Train.

Droitwich Branch Canal Junction

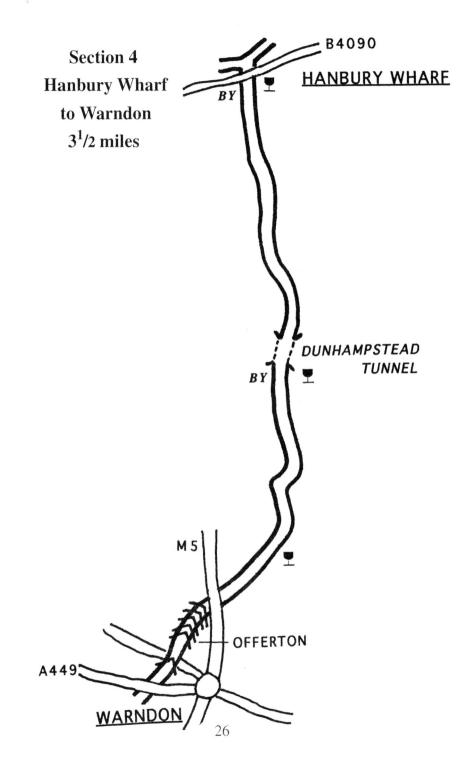

Section 4
Hanbury Wharf
to Warndon
3^{1}/2 miles

B4090

HANBURY WHARF

BY

DUNHAMPSTEAD
TUNNEL

BY

M5

OFFERTON

A449

WARNDON

26

For a small centre, Hanbury Marina has much to offer to the boat crews. Food and drink (already mentioned), also a chandlery, for any item concerning narrow boats, a good mooring, and the opportunity to look at the renovation work being carried out on the Droitwich Canal.

Just beyond the Marina, on the far side of the water, there is a lengthy wooden walkway running for some considerable distance,where upwards of 25 boats are moored. There are small but well cared-for gardens, and it is obvious that most of the boats are permanently moored there. In some ways it is reminiscent of the house-boats along the canals in Amsterdam.

As has already been seen during our walk, many of the names painted on the craft are imaginative, and humorous. There are also several which originate from freight carrying vessels, now converted for dwellings. They appear to be comfortable and roomy, and some are in the process of renovation or re-painting.

We now pass under bridges 34 and 33, and as we approach the latter, we can see Hadzor House to the West, and also the outskirts of Droitwich. The house contains the offices and research centre for a large pharmaceutical company, and is imposing from three sides. The original house was built for the Galton family around 1779, and therefore pre-dates the Birmingham - Worcester by some twenty or so years. Prior to being converted to commercial use, it was a school, with possibly religious connections.

During our most recent walk, a handwritten notice, requesting boat crews to slow down because of bank repair work, was seen on the far side, but the state of that section of towpath suggest that the work has been completed. However, the fact that the top of the bank is only about six inches above normal water level makes sense of such a request.

A Duck and seven small ducklings swims past on the far side of the waterway, giving added pleasure to all canal users. There are reeds in this area which add to both beauty, and to the security of any wildlife, though they tend to narrow the navigable channel, thus reducing speed even further at busy periods. The world of the canal boat is leisurely anyway, and no-one seems to mind the occasional need to give way. Where the reeds form a solid wall along the path, views over the water are restricted, and Anglers find it necessary to make a spot to place their equipment.

Bridge no. 32, is now reached. It is marked on the map as "Hammonds Bridge", and is a farm access, with walking width only. On one visit, this was suitable for taking a Lunch break, and following scrambling up a slippery slope to reach the structure's centre, a very pleasant panorama was revealed. Fields stretched away to the Eastward, firstly bordering the railway line, just visible, then continuing toward the lovely village of Himbleton. Not practical for the walker to try and reach from the waterway, but well worth a visit on another day. To the North-West, a half timbered building, with Elizabethan chimneys attracts the eye, and with a good lens, presents a good photographic opportunity. The map seems to imply that this is a farm but the absence of other buildings, and machinery give rise to doubt on that point.

Several boats pass under the bridge, their respective crews waving a now anticipated greeting up at the bridge. The bridge itself is not subject to much weight, and it may well be that the brickwork has not been replaced over the years.

Down the slippery slope, and back on the towpath, cottages can be seen a short way ahead, just around a small bend. Trees all around them border the bridge, no. 31. This is the hamlet of Shernal Green. The cottages have pretty gardens, the road over the bridge carries more agricultural traffic than commercial, and the few minutes needed to look at the area, is well worth the small effort involved. In many ways, the community is very like some of the villages along the Norfolk Broads, although most of the time, the waterway is much less busy. Horses crossing the bridge, and birds singing in the hedges make the scenario complete.

A few paces beyond Shernal Green, and the sound of passing trains brings us back into the twentieth century, although they are too far away to be very intrusive. There are fields on either side and the water curves to the right, at which point trees line the banks. Just ahead is another tunnel entrance, complete with towpath sloping upward and away from the canal. This is the Dunhampstead Tunnel, a mere

236 yards in length, or whatever that is in metres. We pass the tunnel entrance, and enter a small wood, still on a firm path. Several farms are seen on the land over the now invisible waterway, the first bearing the obvious title "Tunnel Farm". During Spring, the driveway up to that farm is lined with Daffodils, and various shrubs add to the pleasant grounds.

Very soon, we are descending back to the water, from where we see Dunhampstead wharf. Here there is a busy boatyard, Brookline Boats, and along the path, a good mooring for boaters. There are also parking facilities, a small shop, and the Fir Tree Inn, offering mementos of one's visit, or food and drink, whichever may be required. Just out of view from the waterside, there are tasteful cottages, and other pleasant country walks.

We have just passed under a road bridge (no. 30), and there are more moorings, this time permanent ones. The scene now opens out into rural Worcestershire at it's best. There are a few reeds on the far side, and although no lock, an overflow takes excess water into the nearby stream. The railway is getting nearer again, having crossed Dunhampstead via a level crossing, but all else is pure countryside. There are more Ducks, and a few Moorhens along this section, but this is also a stretch where you can hope to see a Heron. He is very happy to stand in the fields along the far side, and is not scared away by express trains. However, moving Cattle, or severe noise of an unfamiliar nature sends him flying low to another vantage point one or two fields away. When the grass is long, you need to look very carefully, for he makes little or no movement unless disturbed. In Spring, Cuckoos are seen and heard in this area, and have several trees near to the towpath where they rest.

Bridge no. 29 is passed, then, as we reach no. 28, the railway is at our shoulder. Quite literally, since it is a mere dozen yards away and higher than the path. We have now reached Oddingley.

Over to the right, is the Parish Church of St. James, Oddingley. It is a very different architecture from most of our Parish Churches. The Tower has a somewhat Saxon style in shape and form, although the present building (having had major repairs in the nineteenth century) was built in the fifteenth century.

Near to the Church is a half-timbered house, once a farm, now a most picturesque home.

There are Cattle and Sheep in the surrounding fields, and hoofprints on the towpath remind us of the time when narrow boats were towed by Horses or Mules.

The steep camber of the railway tracks, and the high speed of the trains can be a little intimidating, at this point, but regular walking along this section ultimately enables one to truly relax, and just enjoy the thrill of seeing express passenger trains at close quarters.

Several times the canal widens, then narrows again for another bridge.

There are still reedy stretches, but mostly two boats can pass each other along much of the section. The sheltered towpath makes it a popular venue for fishermen.

Our next contact with a community comes at Tibberton, where, after passing beneath bridge 25, we see the Bridge Public House, together with a large car park, also a road and several houses. We have been within earshot of the M5 Motorway for a little while, so it is not really surprising that we very shortly reach a very modern bridge, carrying that road over the waterway. Though it is a large structure, it is not out of keeping with it's surroundings, and very close by, is a modern farm. We also see the first lock for some little distance, which is in fact the first in a group of six taking us once again into open countryside.

The descent is alongside Smite hill, close to the hamlet of Smite, where another of Worcestershires popular country eating places "The Pear Tree" is situated.

Bridge 24 is passed, and to the right we see for the first time the imposing building of Hindlip Hall.

Hindlip Hall is the headquarters of the West Mercia Constabulary, and has been considerably enlarged to accommodate the many facets of a large Police authority. However, the original house on this site, and it's replacement, were very much immersed in the history of, not only the County, but also the Country.

Built in the reign of Elizabeth 1st, the first house was destroyed by fire. The rebuilt mansion figured prominently in the 'Gunpowder

Plot', and in fact, some of the main conspirators were captured there in 1606.

Later, Allsopps, the noted brewing family enlarged the house in 1867, and it was during these alterations that a chest, containing notes about the great families of the county, and buried during the English Civil War, was discovered. These notes had been compiled by one Thomas Habington, and after discovery, they were published in 1895. They can now be found in the Worcester Library.

Close to the Offerton Bottom Lock, the last in this group, there is access to a variety of roads. There is the M5 Motorway, the A449 feeder road, also roads which lead to Droitwich or Evesham, and others lead to Blackpole or Warndon, the former mainly industrial and the other with a large number of houses. Here too, is 'Six Ways', the home of Worcester Rugby Union Football Club, whose ground has recently been modernised and upgraded, with the Club now playing a higher grade of Rugby.

Our section ends here, and as is always the case, there is a choice of returning to Hanbury Marina, or finding Public Transport, although it may require a further walk in order to reach a Bus route into the City.

Country Lock - Tibberton

Section 5   Warndon to Diglis Basin, Worcester
5 Miles.

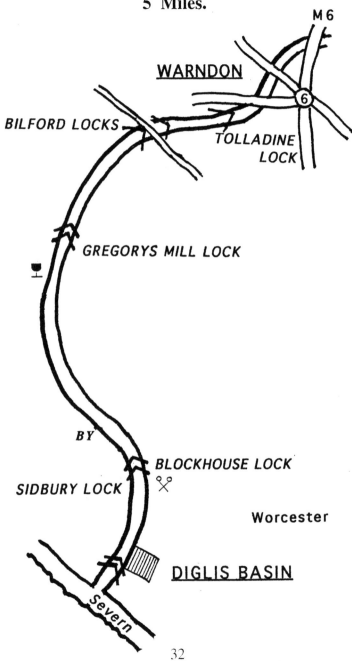

For those who begin a walk from 'Six Ways', there are a few parking places in Smite lane, which runs from the A4538 Droitwich road. However, access to the towpath is either from near the lock cottage, further up toward the canal bridge at Smite, or via the narrow lane running to the right of the Rugby ground. Whichever is chosen, there will be up to five locks to walk down past, then bridge no. 23 to pass beneath the A4538, or alternatively there will be a short flat walk toward the modern bridge carrying the A449 feeder. This section of canal is both wide and level, and the condition of the path, excellent. When I first walked this stretch, some fourteen years ago, the towpath was so bad that it was necessary to walk down the lane for over one hundred yards. In keeping with almost every section walked, for the purposes of this book, the state of towpaths is much improved. In fact, the worst one finds is that the surface is the original one, with mud and puddles in places, but not eroded to a point where one cannot progress.

This is another popular spot for fishermen, and I can understand them appreciating the pleasant surroundings, as well as their sport

The bridge to which we now get closer, is, of necessity, large, but there is an added point of interest there. That is the triangular stone which marks the boundary of the City of Worcester, although we still have some way to go before before we reach the City Centre. Placed within a wooden framework, also triangular, the stone bears the simple inscription City of Worcester, together with the Coat of Arms.

Once under the bridge, the waterway is narrower, and one of the most predominant features in view, is the Radio Mast at Hindlip Hall, also part of the building itself, although in Summer, a tree shields some of the Hall from view.

Deep reed beds cover the bank on the far side, and the water runs gently through a right hand curve. A few yards further on, there is a bridge no. 22, it being merely a farm footbridge, and carries no vehicles. Here, the towpath reverts to its original surface, which means that here and there, there are muddy patches, after rain. British Waterways can be excused for the few sections where the walking surface is below standard, for they have large areas to cover in their maintenance schedule. It merely means that the walker should be prepared to wear stronger footwear than in some other sections.

We have another straight stretch, and there is a Spinney to the edge of the path. We pass under another little used bridge a little way beyond Tolladine Lock, this is no. 21. From here the Blackpole Trading Estates are close by our left side, whilst across open fields, can be seen and heard, the A449 feeder road, as it runs parallel at that point.

Watching the various workers on the business park reminds me of a passage from 'Three Men in a Boat' by Jerome K Jerome, "I like work, it fascinates me, I can sit and look at it for hours".

Just prior to the next lock 'Blackpole No 9', the canal widens once more, following the cessation of earlier banks of reeds, and there appears to have been a bridge, since removed in the section. This possibility is borne out by the absence of the number 20, since our next bridge is no. 19, and follows the lock very swiftly. We notice that a new pedestrian access has been placed nearby, from close to the retail park, also at Blackpole. In good weather, this is a bonus for staff from this area, who enjoy a quiet, peaceful stroll in their lunch hours.

The next feature we reach, is bridge no. 18, which conveys the railway line into the City from Birmingham or Kidderminster. Just beyond, is no. 17, from where we see a new housing estate to our left, and a wide expanse of sports field, to our right. This is the start of the huge amenity complex of Perdiswell, which includes Sports hall, Concert hall, and many other modern facilities. Along this section, Swans are seen, together with Cygnets (in season), also local people enjoying the open aspect, or just walking their dogs.

There is some mooring here, but this is mainly for those heading for the next lock Bilford top lock no. 8, which fronts a main road bridge and is close to several Schools. Near to the lock, is a modern home, created from an earlier lock cottage, but now, apart from it's position, has no connection with the waterway.

The road bridge is no. 15 and we pass beneath, descending into a quiet wide area of canal, shortly leading to Bilford bottom lock no. 7. At this point, the towpath is wide and well maintained, a really good walking surface all the way to our final destination. There are houses to our left, and reedy banks on the right. A very straight waterway runs toward bridge no. 14, a footbridge which connects to the towpath directly. Many of the houses, which are below water level, have gates onto the towpath, and beyond the high hedges and reeds, there are some buildings which appear to be flats. There are many ducks and moorhens here, also a family of Swans which use the far bank to rest their legs after a morning swim. Beyond the houses, there is a sports field which can be seen through gaps in the hedge, and we are already nearing the next lock. This is no. 6, Gregorys Mill top lock, which is in the middle of a wide length of canal. Trees line both sides, at this point, to make a sheltered peaceful walk.

Gregorys Mill bottom lock (no. 5) is only a short distance further on, and immediately an old metal footbridge carries the towpath to the west side of the waterway. and us with it.

There is now much evidence of an Industrial area, on both sides, and the bridge we have recently crossed, is much used by workers heading for their daily stint. Incidentally, this is the first time since Tardebigge that the towpath has run along the Western edge.

We can now see the floodlight gantries at Worcester City (Association) Football ground, as we follow the water in a gentle left hand curve. The canal is still wider than many stretches, and remains so for much of the remainder of it's length.

At the end of the football ground, we find the "Cavalier Tavern", which claims that " Canal Boats and Fishermen are welcome". My peculiar sense of humour is trying to work out how one gets a Canal Boat inside a pub, but one realises what they mean. Moorings are readily available at this point.

We are reminded by this Tavern, of the English Civil War, and the fact that the Worcester City coat of arms carries the word 'Faithful', a reference to the loyalty of the City to the Crown, during these troubled years. Worcester was, of course, involved twice in the war, the first time at an early skirmish at Powick Bridge, where Prince Rupert defeated a small force of Round-head troops, then at the very end of the second civil war, when Prince Charles (later to become King Charles 11) just managed to escape from Cromwells superior force. The event is commemorated in a plaque on one of the older buildings in the City centre.

However, back to the latter part of the twentieth century. The bridge near the Tavern no. 12, is another road bridge, and is a busy route into the centre. The waterway is straight with hedges and trees, and some gardens reach down to the waterside by terraces which are colourful. To the right is Flagge Meadow, a sporting complex for the Worcester Royal Grammar School, followed shortly by a large public park.

We have passed below bridge no. 11, the waterway swings gently to the right, and over the water is a very large allotment area. Updated terraced properties, along, or at the end of various roads, are on the edge of the towpath, though the allotments continue on the left.

We can now see bridge no. 10, another railway carrier, and on reaching this construction, notice that where the roadway passes through a single track arch, just above is a large circular hole, running the whole width of the bridge. It is at least high enough for a person to pass standing upright, and it's exact purpose is not clear. We think it may be connected with the passage of air through the very thick structure, but that is mere conjecture.

For a few seconds, we leave the canal side, to walk over a humped bridge flanking the entrance to the Viking Boatyard. This is one of the larger of the yards on the Birmingham-Worcester, and is always worth a stop to watch the boats which are not currently cruising.

Then it is back onto the towpath and under bridge no. 9, carrying traffic from Rainbow Hill, into Lowesmoor. There are stylish flats at this point, and to the left can be seen Shrub Hill Trading Estate, and other industry. Almost at once, we pass under bridge no. 8, which actually links Shrub Hill with the City Centre.

There is now another long straight stretch, with commercial buildings lining both sides to quite a height. Bridge no. 7 seems to have been spirited away, for the footbridge we now reach, is no. 6.

We make a final crossing of the water, at bridge no. 5, near St. Martins, and here there are new houses, as well as some industry. We once more negotiate a wide right hand curve, during which we are overhung by Willow trees, as is the far bank. Lock no. 4, together with bridge no. 4, at Blockhouse offers a sight of the Cathedral tower, and just around the next left turn we see the Commandery. This building, or rather complex, housed the Royalist Headquarters during the Civil War, and now has a museum which is not to be missed, unless one has no interest whatever in the history of our country. There are many interesting features here, also a shop and cafe, ironically titled Cromwells Pantry. The district is Sidbury, and lock and bridge, both numbered three, are right alongside the road. Just across the road, is the premises of Worcester Royal Porcelain, with museum and cafe, another very well worthwhile stop.

Having passed under Sidbury, the canal is at it's narrowest for some distance, passing between industrial premises on the way to Diglis Basin. Very soon, however the waterway widens to accommodate many moored craft, and as we pass beneath the factory road of bridge no. 2, we reach the basin itself.

A wealth of different boats, some much larger than those seen on our canal walk, are dotted around two basins, and we walk between the two to reach the locks taking craft onto the river Severn. On the far side is a lock-keepers cottage. This time a real working one, with a lock keeper available. There is a dry dock similar in construction to the one at Stourport.

Two locks only, remain. Diglis top lock, and Diglis bottom lock, both much bigger than we have seen previously, for all craft entering or leaving the river, must pass through them.

Our walk along the Worcester & Birmingham Canal is ended. Once more, the choice to retrace steps, or to use Public Transport faces us, however, there is also a third choice for the energetic. A wander through the City of Worcester, or along the river bank. I hear you saying " That is for another day, thank you".

We have walked (in stages) through the beautiful Worcestershire countryside, with as wide a variety of Geographical features, Natural History, and different views, as could possibly be imagined.

I hope to be able to walk these various routes for some years to come, for I find every walk to be different, and the whole process to be therapeutic, as well as interesting.

Bilford Top Lock

Winter Morning approaching Worcester

Part Two

The Staffordshire and Worcestershire Canal

Section 1 Stourport to Wolverley 6 miles.

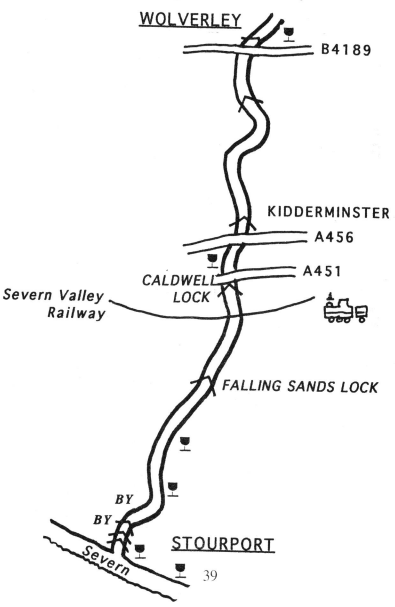

WOLVERLEY

B4189

KIDDERMINSTER

A456

A451

CALDWELL
LOCK

Severn Valley
Railway

FALLING SANDS LOCK

BY

BY

STOURPORT

Severn

After his success in designing the Bridgwater Canal, James Brindley was commissioned to carry out a similar task for a waterway to link the river Severn with more Northerly rivers, such as the Trent and the Mersey. We would probably have raised our eyebrows at this choice, for Brindley was a mender of machinery by trade, and poorly educated, even by the standards of the 1760's. However, having made a success of his earlier work, he was asked to lay out the route for this new venture, which, it was hoped, would serve the industrial interests of Midland companies. Perhaps, even then, the industrial revolution could be envisaged, although at the time, there was a certain amount of risk that the new system of transport might not provide all the answers.

Brindley arrived in Worcestershire in 1765, and was immediately faced with the problem of where the link with the Severn was to be made. The most obvious choice was Bewdley, due to it's well established trading base and light manufacturing capability. Unfortunately, the hilly terrain between Kidderminster and Bewdley was against the Brindley method of canal design, that is by using the natural ground contours, following river valleys where possible, thus avoiding the need for multiple locks, and excessive rock blasting. The citizens of Bewdley, contrary to popular belief, wanted the canal to reach the river via their town, but it became necessary to re-think the situation.

As a result of careful deliberation, and in line with his policy of following natural features, in this case the river Stour, Brindley decided to build his junction at a village called Lower Mitton, which was subsequently re-named Stourport. As history will show, this has developed into more than a waterway interchange, and is a centre for manufacturing and industry in it's own right.

Having selected the point at which the new canal would join with the river Severn, work on the project began at the highest point on the whole route, namely Compton, in Staffordshire.

This new waterway, together with new sections, such as the Stourbridge Canal (designed by others), was largely responsible for the rapid growth of Midland industry, the most noted area becoming known as 'The Black Country'.

The success of the Staffordshire & Worcestershire, and indeed of many canals, was somewhat eroded by the railway boom of the mid nineteenth century, and also by improving roads. In fact, were it not for the value of their service during the two European Wars, they might well have been lost to the inhabitants of Great Britain as a result of disuse. They were allowed to silt up, and to fall into disrepair, but thanks to the long-sightedness of small groups of the public, and the efforts of the Inland Waterway Association and British Waterways, we now have two thriving cruising businesses, Severn Valley Cruisers and Stroudwater Cruisers, and an interest which ensures proper maintenance.

The canal was completed in 1772, at a cost of £100,000, though sadly Brindley died the same year without seeing the final results of his labours. It bears many typical Brindley features, and the Stourport basin is large by comparison with others. On the Southern edge is The 'Tontine' Hotel, which in various form has existed throughout the canal era. Narrow boats entering from the Severn, need to cross right across the basin in order to start the journey along all or part of the Staffs/Worcs.

We pass under part of.the town's 'One-Way' system, through a very narrow lock, and on through the main visitor moorings parallel to High Street, and Lion Hill. Original warehouses have been demolished to make way for a modern development of Town Houses, though some of the original walls remain on this stretch. The towpath here has been updated in recent years, and is very walkable, providing a varied view of the rear of shop premises in Lombard Street. A new footbridge follows the road bridge in the middle of the moorings, near to which the Black Star pub offers food and drink for travellers.

The waterway bears sharp right, under the Lower Mitton road bridge, straightens for a hundred yards or so, before turning in the other direction under Gilgal (no. 6) footbridge which links the road at Gilgal with St. Michael's Church, and Churchyard. Here, sandstone rocks can be seen for the first of many times, and we now enter another quite lengthy straight. A pair of white cottages at the edge of the towpath bear an inscription stating that they were built in 1800 to give housing to canal Builders. This might suggest that even after it's original opening, there was still work to be done along the waterway.

A few yards further on stands the 'Bird in Hand', a modernised, but unspoilt, and very popular public house. This is as well used by locals, as well as visiting boats.

A few feet away, on the far side, stands a gigantic brick wall with mooring rings, but no access path. This marks the edge of a freight wharf, situated where the railway once crossed the canal over a bridge which now leads to a countryside park. There is also a small inlet where boats could be loaded or unloaded, and which was used in conjunction with the railway. A modern housing estate covers the site of the old track, in a townward direction, but along the path, where we walk, buildings have ended for now.

There are still some properties (a mixture of old and new), on the far side, but low lying fields contain the meandering Stour, which is visible from time to time. Beyond these fields can be seen the area of Wilden, where there are a number of properties, a Church, and an Industrial Estate, built on the site of the former Richard Thomas & Baldwins steel works.

We pass beneath a bridge which once carried vehicles, but is now restricted to pedestrians and horses.

The waterway swings to the left, then to the right, and all houses are behind us. A group of Horses, belonging to a local riding school graze on the high banks to the left, and Anglers can be seen all along this section where the path is wide and mainly weed free. The surface of the towpath, however is original, and a little subject to muddy patches.

Shortly, where the canal once more swings to the right, we reach bridge no. 8 at Bonemill, from where there is access to the main Kidderminster road. As the water follows the natural contours of the land, we note that ground is high to the left, but low-lying to the right. Because of the risk of flooding from the river, there are no crops in the fields toward Wilden, just Cattle and Horses.

The canal is less winding between Bonehill and the next bridge at Oldington (no. 9).

At Oldington, there is a large trading estate which is mainly hidden from the canal, but vehicles seeking company premises frequently come over the narrow bridge. When they find nothing except a narrow lane, they retrace their steps and leave the waterway to Walkers, Anglers, and solitude.

We now continue towards Kidderminster, and where the canal widens, we are at the rear of the British Sugar Corporation. It is only local knowledge which tells us this fact, for there are no signs of the factory. A humped back bridge takes us over a stream, and trees line both sides of the water. A few yards further on, there is a lock, the first since Stourport. Nearby is an overflow which is unlike the typical Brindley design, being merely a simple ramp with a low lip. Brindley's overflows are largely a square brick-built open box, with a central metal grille which traps large items such as tree branches, and which can then be easily cleared. The grille is domed, and the overall effect is as of a 'plughole'. Such a construction is seen frequently on the Staffs/Worcs.

From the lock, the area known as 'Hoobrook' can be seen. This is mainly an industrial area, though there are some tall flats there. A high viaduct now crosses the canal, and is worth examining. It is quite high, and carries the Severn Valley Railway which, prior to the infamous Dr Beeching, carried Sugar Beet to the aforementioned factory, also passengers from Kidderminster to either Bridgnorth or Tenbury. It is now in regular use by the 'New' Severn Valley Railway which was rescued from obscurity by a group of far-seeing enthusiasts during the 1960's. This section was opened in 1984 and links Kidderminster and Bewdley and is largely Steam hauled. It also connects with British Rail at Kidderminster. Many thousands of visitors, both National and International have visited the railway thus putting the area well and truly on the map.

At this point, the canal narrows considerably, and runs between a high bank on the left, where houses perch precariously above a screen of trees, and business units which flank the towpath. Here, there is another lock which has an iron footbridge to assist boat crews to operate the paddles on the far side. This is called Caldwell Lock. Crossing the water next, is a modern road bridge (no. 13 Round Hill) referring to a large natural feature which lies to the left, just beyond a right hand bend. It is only a few yards before a bridge carrying only an access lane is negotiated. The road joining this lane is entitled Tram Street. This refers to the location of a Tram Depot, in the early part of the century, when those vehicles carried workers to and from Stourport.

We are now in the industrial section of Kidderminster, and just past 'Castle Road' bridge we enter 'The Sling' where I first walked along canals. On the far side is Park Lane, where a large Timber Merchant has premises, but along much of the towpath are the former buildings of Brintons, world famed Carpet manufacturers, although they are in the process of relocating outside the town centre.

We climb over a humped bridge, still on the towpath, which once took materials into and out of Brintons premises, and opposite which, there is a 'winding hole', an area for turning narrow boats. Only the main channel is deep enough for navigation.

We now pass between high brick walls, turning right to face a deep lock and bridge which is under part of the Inner Ringroad. The gates are covered with growing plants and have been in place for many years. Prior to the road being changed, the canal flowed beneath a severe humped-back bridge, just beyond which were several Lock Cottages. There was also a wharf, from where St. Mary's Parish Church could just be seen. After clearance of the canal buildings, the view of the Church is now very open.

St. Mary's, standing as it does on high ground, makes an imposing sight, and is well worth a visit, both from it's architecture, and also the historical value. When the ring road was constructed, the Church was isolated from the town centre. Later, the marbled statue of Richard Baxter a non-conformist preacher was moved to the area immediately in front of the main entrance to the Parish Church.A step in the direction of reconciliation between Churches was brought about. Kidderminster has another claim to fame, that is as the birthplace of Rowland Hill, creator of the 'Penny Post'.

The river Stour, which has been on a parallel course since Stourport, now passes beneath the canal, by means of a small aqueduct. From this feature, the comparative shallowness of canals can be judged. Through broad sweeps, the waterway runs through Clensmore, once a thriving industrial part of the town, now a shadow of it's former self. The towpath here is surfaced with Tarmac, and is wide enough for heavy vehicles to pass, but soon reverts to normal surface as the derelict buildings are passed.

There is evidence of a former bridge at this point, since the canal narrows to a few feet, however, most of the local dog walkers remain on the far side.

Anglers use this stretch, and not only human ones, for Kingfishers flash across the water, their brilliant irridescence being both unmistakable and colourful. On one occasion, one of these wonderful birds was perched on a overhanging branch, just feet away from a human fisher who had either not noticed, or become used to their presence.

Tree-lined, and wide at this point,there is a path on the far side, though not a towpath in the original sense of the phrase.

We are now out of the town, though modern housing estates can still be seen to both sides. Immediately to our sides, are large uncultivated fields, and the odd Willow tree, but very little more.

We soon reach Wolverley Court bridge, and lock. The name refers to a large white building away to the right, and through trees, can be seen the spire of St. John's Church, Wolverley. We are rapidly approaching the bridge and then the Lock at Wolverley itself. Sandstone rock on the right, gives way to a modern, but tasteful glass extension to a private house. Hard by the lock is The 'Lock Inn', known for it's food and drink, also for Music which has become part of it's function. There are good moorings for the narrow boat users, and a good vantage point for "Gongoozlers". What a wonderful word. It simply means people who stand and watch canal boats, and their manoeuvrings.

We have reached the end of the section, and six miles may be a little too much for an immediate return walk. There are buses to Kidderminster, if one has a timetable.

Stourport Basin

Wolverley in Winter

Section 2 Wolverley to Stourton 6$\frac{1}{2}$ miles

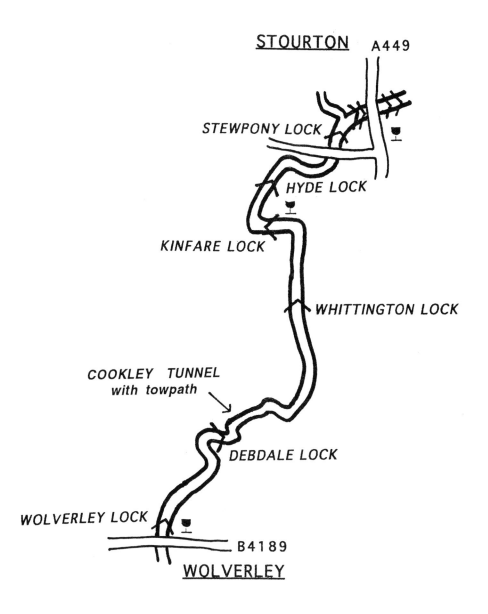

STOURTON   A449

STEWPONY LOCK

HYDE LOCK

KINFARE LOCK

WHITTINGTON LOCK

COOKLEY TUNNEL
with towpath

DEBDALE LOCK

WOLVERLEY LOCK

B4189

WOLVERLEY

Before commencing a walk from Wolverley, one should admire the scenery at this beautiful spot. It has provided many with the inspiration for both painting and Photography, and at most times of the year, private or cruise boats offer colour for both purposes.

The towpath follows a tree-lined section, with high banks to the right, and open views (beyond trees) to the left. From here we can easily see the Church of St. John, already referred to, also other properties including Wolverley House away in the trees to the North-West. Now divided into flats, it was in the late 1940's a boarding house for Sebright School. I attended it for two years, so this view brings back many memories.

Across the water, the narrow winding road from Wolverley to Cookley follows the canal contours, a lengthy brick wall shadowing it. This wall forms the boundary of the Lea Castle estates, now subdivided by main roads, and without any castle. There are several properties along the water, each with private moorings. In some cases, these are modernised cottages, in others purpose-built homes.

We pass under bridge no. 16, taking good care to check for any cyclists, since this is a very blind spot on the towpath. There are not many water birds in evidence, probably the absence of reeds means no nest sites or hiding places, but the ubiquitous Blackbirds, Robins, and Wrens frequent the hedgerows, and from the woodlands to the West, the occasional call of a Pheasant may be heard. In Spring, Cuckoos add to the sound of the countryside, and Rhododendrons colour the banks under the emerging leaves of overhanging trees.

Now, there is a wide expanse of water, and a few reeds appear along the far edge. The Cookley-bound road continues to wind it's way as if it is reluctant to leave the canalside, but eventually it rises up towards St. Peter's Church, passing Sports fields on the way, and we are out of sight of vehicles for a while.

The only lock for some little distance now appears just ahead, and with it a lock cottage. There is a footbridge to assist operators of the lock, and as we draw level, the early signs of Cookley village can be seen This is Debdale Lock.

There are farms, a riding school, and many horses to the left, also obstacles for riders to learn the art of jumping over fences. A large industrial complex appears as if engulfing the towpath, but on reaching the factory wall, we see that the path crosses a metal bridge whilst skirting the buildings. No doubt, at one time this bridge allowed water into the factory premises, although it is very clear that it has long since been blocked to boat traffic.

As we follow the contour of the waterway to the right, we see the dark and forbidding blackness of a tunnel. This runs under the main road of the village for a number of yards,. but there is a towpath alongside, together with a handrail, so no restrictions to walking through. In wet weather, be aware that there may be puddles along the path, and drips of water coming from the tunnel roof.

At either end of this brief cover, there are paths leaving the canal for the Public Houses and shops in Cookley. One of those Pubs has a small private mooring, and a direct stairway to it's premises.

Once out into the daylight again, sandstone rocks form the right bank of the waterway, whilst low fields border the towpath. Shortly, we see the caravan park at Austcliffe, also on the right. This is a mixture of temporary and permanent homes, all in immaculate condition, and well laid out, so that it blends with the surroundings. It is exactly the type of site that I would be happy to live on, for it has a homely feel.

We are now heading towards Caunsall, which begins where Cookley ends. This stretch is another very popular with Fishermen, and we need to avoid their rods, creels, and tins of wriggling bait, but they are always tolerant of other towpath users, and move any obstructions on our approach. We are greeted with cheery 'Good Mornings' or whatever the appropriate time of day it may be, and probably a reference to the prevailing weather.

Water Voles have been seen, swimming from one bank to another, but these little creatures seem to have been reduced in number in recent years. Overhead, Rooks are always busy, according to seasonal requirements, whether it be collecting nesting materials or food. Despite the low banks and hedges, there is something of an enclosed feeling as we near the next bridge.

Amateur and Professional Artists have been known to use this part of the canal, and the occasional Easel can be seen on the edge of the path. There are parking places near this bridge, which links Cookley & Caunsall with the A449 trunk route, it might therefore prove to be a good starting/finishing point for some walkers.

The water winds gently through this shaded area, which is the start of one of the many very pretty stretches of the Staffs/Worcs. On a never to be forgotten day in Summer 1998, we started to walk from this point, and the sun filtered through the overhanging trees making patterns on both water and earth. A hundred yards along the far bank, there was a familiar figure. Standing in the water, gazing intently with sharp eye, was a Heron. This one was an adult, and his reflection made him look really large. I crept forward, camera in hand, hoping to get the photograph of a lifetime, before he took flight. Like an idiot, I had not replaced the film, so with my last shot, I needed to ensure speed, exposure, and lens were all perfect. Shaking hands do not help at such a juncture, and the mediocre result did not surprise me.

Shortly after taking the shot, he flew away, not due to my presence, but because two narrow boats were approaching from the other direction. During that walk, I had nine sightings of Herons, quite a remarkable happening, though I never discovered how many were sightings of one bird, however, it is my guess that there were several, for the length of the walk made that more likely. I headed the page in my notebook, "Herons all the Way".

The waterway swings to the left, creating the optical illusion that the trees on both sides are merging. The quiet, after the boats had passed, was noticeable, and once more we can see the river, on parallel course a short distance to the West. Fields with sheep, also a small number of young cattle, occupy some fields beyond the river, and a blue sheen identifies a crop of Linseed creating a colourful horizon. Our friend the Heron made his second appearance here.

The canal winds leisurely on, and along the far bank is the trunk of an old Oak tree, from which small branches and the green of it's leaves indicate there is still life within. It partly obstructs the channel, but adds character to the rural scene.

The diminutive form of a 'Jenny' Wren flits among the foliage, near the towpath, making the sort of high volume of noise one would have expected from a much larger bird.

A solid wall of sandstone rock, on the far side makes us remember the construction process, and we wonder whether Navvies blasted their way through part of this rock, or if it is just a natural escarpment. We recall Brindley always tried to use natural contours, but some of the marks and edges of the sandstone suggest this might have been assisted by Dynamite, at this point.

My attention is drawn to a piece of equipment covered with ivy, at the edge of the path. It looks like a ratchet controlling a sluice which would have been used to drain excess water into the river. Obviously not used for some years, it is doubtful if it could now be operated, even if there were an emergency.

British Waterways workmen were preparing to reinforce the bank on the left side, and had left bundles of metal edgings for that purpose. Despite the need for them to carry out the work, they ensure that the materials cause little or no hinderance for the walker. At the risk of repetition, I cannot praise this organisation too highly, for the way in which so much of our waterways have been restored.

The rock has now given way to fields which now line the far bank,and there are a few patches of reed. A Heron rises from the towpath, flies over the water, and settles at the edge of a field. Just below his vantage point, a gaggle of Canada Geese graze beneath a tree, each species respecting the other. These are the first Geese seen on this water, and the scarcity of such birds on canals suggest that they prefer open stretches of water, from which they can fly easily to safety, should danger threaten. Later, on our return, they swim as in a flotilla, leaving 'V' ripples across the surface.

To the right, there is the new sight of a private garden, which extends along the water's edge toward the next bridge (no. 27) at Whittington, and it's accompanying lock. A steep path to the lane running over the bridge, replaces the towpath which usually passes beneath. We climb to the summit, pass through a gateway, and are by the lockside. On the far side stands a modernised, and extended lock cottage, and a boat descends within the confines of the lock. Several other boats wait their turn to follow, and we once more notice that the crews not only converse, but assist each other. The sight of a wooden seat, constructed from old lock gate timbers suggests that it is time for refreshment, and with this, there can be no argument. We also have a good view of the descending boats.

The relaxed attitude, and lack of rancour, from the holidaying crews, is such a contrast to the modern 'road rage', even though there are times when a delay occurs through 'heavy' traffic. Our waterways can he thought to be therapeutic.

The seat on which I have been sitting bears a dedication to a former chairman of a local canal society, and refers to the dedication of such persons in the preservation or restoration of the canals. Their foresight and efforts have resulted in our ability to walk in the peace of our waterways.

A modernised property, adjacent to the towpath, is in character with the canal, much of the front being covered with flowers, and has a swimming pool at the rear which looks tempting in the morning sun. A weeping Willow over the path has to be brushed aside for progress to be made, but we are relaxed, enjoying the wonders of nature and pleased with the beauty of all trees.

Behind a hedge are Chickens, Ducks, and Geese, all free-running, and at the next cottage, free range eggs are available. This cottage, or rather pair of cottages, is quite old, and has a wonderful garden complete with roses and other Summer flowers, typical of an English country property.

Vegetables are on sale, along with the eggs, but a notice 'Beware of the Dog', seems like a contradictory statement. As if to reinforce that notice, a large German Shepherd dog stands by the gate, but does not show an aggressive attitude, so perhaps the notice merely suggests that one enters quietly, and shuts the gate.

Approaching another bridge, the canal narrows, and other properties with large gardens stand hard by the water. Under the bridge, the water swings to the left, revealing the far side where two white geese sleep with head under wing. The bridge bears the number 28, but rather surprisingly, the same name as no. 27, Whittington. Quite obviously, this was a 'packhorse bridge', and only allows a walker, or cyclist to cross. It looks like the original brickwork, and one considers the possibility of being the only Whittington bridge, at some time in the past. If that was the case, then the bridge numbers will have been added more recently, for they run consecutively.

Rounding the sharp corner, to pass beneath the structure, we see that dredging has been taking place. Mud and debris has been deposited between the canal edge, and the towpath, so present no obstruction. The items now on display confirm that many stretches of water are still the target for indiscriminate dumping. Bottles, Jars, Cans, pieces of drainpipe, and bricks have been recovered during the operation and their are also some kind of freshwater shellfish, in too great a quantity to have just been thrown from boat. A naturalist would no doubt identify these shells, which are the size of large oysters, and are flat. Possibly fresh-water mussels.

Here, the towpath is original, therefore is muddy in wet weather, and so good footwear is advisable.

We now run alongside small fields, at the edge of which sheep are drinking. The Welsh water pipeline, destined for Birmingham consumers must pass below, at this point, for familiar inspection blocks are below a steep bank.

We are again close to the river, and wild flowers, also colourful weeds grow in profusion on the banks.

Over the water, modernised and extended properties (three close together), share the edges of the canal. Each is nestled within a copse of trees, which include not only the usual broad-leaved Oaks, but also some Yews, and even a 'Monkey Puzzle'. Gardens vary between flowers, and vegetables, scattered between greenhouses and garden sheds. Fruit trees are also evident. What an idyllic place to live! Chattering in the Oak trees are two Jays, presumably searching for any ripened Acorns. Their colour is superb, and they show no signs of fear at the presence of walking humans. They are well worth stopping to watch, but not close enough for a photograph, even if my camera had any film left.

Swinging left, the first signs of Kinver are now seen, firstly from the Kinver Public Mooring signs, then by the increase in properties. Here too, are small paddocks, a walled garden, and other signs of greater habitation by humans, and in the distance, the ubiquitous building of the former Staffordshire waterworks company, now the Severn Trent Ltd.

To the right of the next bridge no. 29, Kinfare, can be seen the Vine public house, complete with signs announcing the availability of food, whilst under a very low arched tunnel can be seen Kinver Lock. Here is a typical Brindley style 'plughole' overflow, a sure sign that we are still on his canal.

The wide, flat moorings above the lock contain several boats, and my information tells me that once, trams ran for a short stretch alongside the waterway. I do not know to what destination.

Along the moorings above Kinver lock, are many narrow boats, some hired, but mostly privately owned. On this day, there was also a metal hulled hulk, for carrying rubbish and dredgings from the water. As is now expected, a former lock cottage stands close by the towpath. It has been modernised, and probably no longer has any connection with the canal, but it is still in keeping with the waterways of the late 1990's.

The water now takes a long sweep to the right, through almost 90 degrees, the moorings continuing throughout. Water and other essential facilities for boat crews are sited here, and in season, visiting craft queue for the various purposes, crews exchanging pleasantries whilst waiting their turn.

After a left turn, the waterway meanders in a gentle manner, but is wide, and very tidily maintained. During the morning walk, the path is bathed in sunshine, but the far side is in shadow, the colours of the trees varying from dark green (in the shade) to an almost springlike hue where the sun catches the upper leaves. We pass Paddock Cottage, which looks like an old lock cottage, both from it's position, and size, but since there is no lock nearby, perhaps it was occupied by a water bailiff, or similar.

At this point, the far banks are rising well clear of the water, but beyond the towpath, the ground drops away into thick undergrowth. The river runs alongside, and is lined by a variety of Silver Birches, Willows, and Oaks. The moorings have finally ended, and the towpath rises steeply up to bridge no. 30, and Hyde lock. The anticipated cottage, has a garden full of young trees, and as is now a matter of frequency, has been more than doubled in size, from the original. Seats have been thoughtfully provided at the edge of the path, within a few yards of the lock, constructed from old tree trunks.

Most locks are pleasant, but the ones which are shaded by green woods and flowers, are ones best remembered, Hyde lock is one such, and called out for a photograph, even though there was no passing boat.

Beyond the lock gates, another large cottage stands near the path, a cottage garden hiding shyly behind the building. Here, the water is straight and wide, and flanked on both sides by woodlands, once the cottage has been passed. On the far side, these woods only continue for about one hundred yards, after which, they 'edge' backward to make way for sloping fields, reaching down to the water's edge. A pair of boats are moored close by each other, and the canal turns firstly to the left, now to the right. On this second bend, five huge Beech trees stand on the very rim of the pathway, their smooth trunks covered with carvings, mainly the initials of passers by. They offer a shady relief from the warmth of the sun, and I expect, in wet conditions, provide appropriate shelter from the rain.

Now, the canal narrows to little more than one boats width, and a renewal of the woods overhang the water giving deep shadow. We are again in bright sunlight, and Bees, Butterflies, and a few Dragonflies soak up the warmth. The river has now retreated several yards distant, but is flanked by Willows, ferns, and many wild flowers.

The waterway is meandering, as if uncertain as to which direction it should follow, and as if by way of explanation for the erratic course, sandstone rock protrudes from beneath the greenery of the far side. Six piles of cemented bricks, each of different height have been placed under one section of rock, supporting, and taking the weight of the natural substance. These were obviously added some time after the original construction.

One more turn in each direction, and a narrow tunnel entrance is in view. This is the short Dunsley Tunnel, a mere twenty five yards in length, but necessitating boats to be moved with plenty of caution. At first sight, this tunnel appears to have been carved out of the local rock, but closer inspection reveals that nature was assisted by the addition of a quantity of bricks. A handrail enables the walker to pass swiftly in safety, and in seconds it is a case of out into the sunlight once more.

The hum of traffic on the A449, can now be heard, as if above the trees across the water, and though sparser, there are still many branches making the far side dark. Looking across the fields to our left, we can see sheep, and pigs, but beyond these, in the trees is the imposing structure of Stourton Castle.

Public moorings are now available, and just beyond, Bridges 31, and 32, both named Stewpony. The first is the main road toward Bridgnorth, the other the pathway just before the lock and wharf.

Information about the immediate section is to be found in the walk along the Stourbridge canal, so I will just say that for the next few yards, until we reach the junction at Stourton bridge, no. 33, there are pleasant moorings on both sides.

Hyde Lock

Section 3 Stourton to Greensforge 4 miles

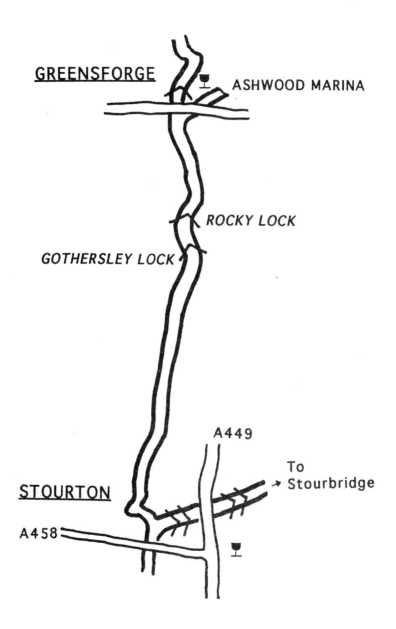

GREENSFORGE   ASHWOOD MARINA

ROCKY LOCK

GOTHERSLEY LOCK

A449

To
Stourbridge

STOURTON

A458

For anyone deciding to start their walk from Stourton, whether it be along the next stretch of the Staffs/Worcs, or along the Stourbridge, there is a parking area just inside the Bridgnorth road, opposite the Stewpony Hotel. At weekends, or bank holidays, it may be necessary to find an alternative.

At the Stourton bridge, there is a signpost, clear and concise. We simply follow the Wolverhampton sign, and almost at once find a very quiet towpath opposite which is private ground. At the first (left hand) bend, there is a large private pool on the far side, usually filled with ducks and geese. On our side is the river, together with lines of poplar trees, making one believe that we might easily be in France. The canal crosses the river, over a bridge which has had reconstruction during the recent decade. Looking along the river, over the far parapet, there is sometimes a Heron standing on the bank, but if not there, careful scanning of the nearby field, may reveal this bird. However, binoculars are advised.

There is a small, but obviously man-made cave just past the bridge and the rock continues for a while. Here and there there a small inlets, temporarily widening the water, but too shallow to allow most craft to enter.

From here to bridge no 34 at Prestwood, the scene varies very little, so far as the nature of the canal is concerned. Most differences on the waterways are produced by the various seasons. For example, the wooded slopes at Prestwood are dotted with purple Rhododendrons in the Spring. I have also walked this stretch in Winter, when three inches of ice covered the waterway from bank to bank, but even then, there was a beauty and tranquillity which made the extra effort worthwhile.

We are now on a very quiet, peaceful and gently winding section of canal, one of the most beautiful along the entire Staffs/Worcs. The woods to the right filter the sunlight onto the surface of the water, whilst away to the left, fallow fields contrast their dull colours against the green of the trees.

Now we reach the site of Gothersley tower, part of a roundhouse built in 1805, and part of an Iron business. Although already in some state of disrepair, the building was occupied until the 1930's. A severe storm finally brought down the remains of the tower in 1991, and all that now remains is a circular wall, some three feet high, with access to a seat, and forming a picnic site.

After a short right curve, we follow a long slow left turn, through the trees to Gothersley bridge (no 35) and lock. Beyond this, the trees have ended, and the waterway is wide. A lane crosses this bridge over which horses and riders can often be seen. We now go into a wide right hand sweep, and find a walled garden with partly hidden house behind. To the left are cultivated fields, on this occasion, in September, Sugar Beet.

Beyond the wall, there is bracken on the far bank, and we can now see Rocky Lock. One of the few patches of reeds here, can now be seen, also a moored boat which looks like a craft on which people live all year round, rather than a holiday boat. There are Ducks waiting for scraps, and the whole area has great atmosphere.

A left turn, past a wild Clematis, and we can see the greenhouses of Ashwood Nurseries. A wood fire burns and crackles in the grounds. There is a tasteful country property between the Nursery buildings and the water. Now, a right turn brings us to Flatheridge bridge (no 36), and we are in sight of the Ashwood Marina. The narrow entrance disguises the size and complexity of this Marina, where hire boats, and private boats taking up much of the vast area. Nearby, Willow trees are in profusion, and once more we see the river close to our towpath.

Just as we pass the first of the moored boats, a Heron takes off from behind them. What an awe-inspiring sight, with wings well spread, legs already tucked up beneath, and the contrasting greys and whites of plumage completing a picture of nature at it's best. A few moments later, and this same bird stands on the path. What a thrill. Two sights together.

Now, we round the final turn before Greensforge.

Quiet Moorings

British Waterways at work - Greensforge

Section 4   Greensforge to Bratch 4³/4 miles

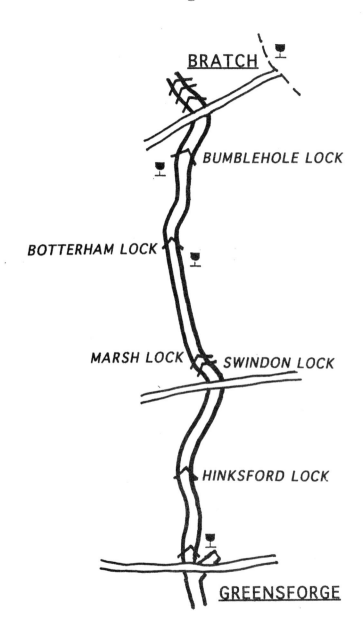

As we have already seen, Ashwood Marina is virtually a branch of it's own, being a large section of waterway, which runs to the right, away from the main channel. In fact, there are several hundred yards separating the Marina from Greensforge itself, something which puzzled me when first I arrived by road.

On the most recent walk, it was a warm Summer morning when I arrived at the 'Navigation' Public House, Greensforge, but I was uncertain whether or not parking would be allowed on their car park. I need not have worried. The licensee, and his good lady were happy to allow my making a start from there, and proved that it always pays to ask permission, and not to assume 'it will be alright'.

Before crossing bridge no 37, to commence the walk, I had a good look at the pub building. It is old, but well maintained, with real atmosphere. Flowers adorned the frontal exterior, and all was clean and tidy.

Later, I was to sample the wares at the 'Navvy', and agreed with many others that the quality of food and drink is high. Alongside the lock, and to the rear of the hostelry, stands a bright lock cottage, with garden full of colour, making a bright day even more colourful. The actual building is typical of it's type. Narrow boats were moving up through the lock, to where water and essential services are available. Other boats waited their turn to negotiate the obstacle, some of them still tethered at the public moorings.

Signs of activity by British Waterway's staff, at the wharf beside the towpath, included unloading dredged materials, and handling the plates for bank reinforcement. However, from the condition of this area, their work would be carried out elsewhere. The workmen were as usual, friendly and cooperative, ensuring that their work, though essential, did not inconvenience other canal users.

The towpath continues on the left hand (or Western) side of the water, and is in excellent condition. No need for Wellington boots here, one could walk right through the section in ordinary shoes. On the far side are sandstone rocks, and above them, trees put down their branches and leaves toward the water, as if trying to obtain a drink. Along the path, the ground drops away into a mass of trees, under which nettles, ferns, and hemlock grow in a tangle.

The waterway is wide, and, once we leave the moorings, curves to the right. There are several fishermen along our bank, and it is most peaceful. Ducks are much in evidence, and though they are nearing adult size, are obviously among those raised this year. Then, as the water curves in the opposite direction, the far side opens out into level fields, and reeds line the edge. They are well controlled, to ensure that boats have sufficient passing space, but still allowing cover for water birds.

There is now a straight section to Hinksford bridge (no 38) and we notice a large caravan park to the left. At the bridge, there is vehicular access to this well laid out site, and a Waterworks building over the water.

Now there is an extended cottage on the far side, with ample room for mooring. Some of the craft look as if they are permanent homes, and several of them are in the course of renovation or repainting. Their various names reveal the strong sense of humour of boating people, an illustration being 'A Nonny Mouse'.

The diminutive narrow boat 'Dawdle', passes us, complete with two humans, and a dog. The gentleman is pouring himself a cup of tea from a teapot, whilst continuing on their way. It could only happen on a boat, or at least one hopes so. Once more, these cruising folk wave cheerily, and we suddenly notice that the caravan park has now finished.

As the waterway begins a very long curve to the left (it does in fact turn through nearly ninety degrees), there is a small section of extra special reinforcement over the far bank. It is more typical of such work alongside roads, in that it consists of banks of large stones held tightly inside netting of metal. At the far end of the curve there is a small bridge which looks original. This is no 39, and through the arch can be seen a pair of quite old lock gates. This is Hinksford Lock, and the entrance to it looks even narrower than usual. The furthest lock gate has been replaced recently. This is a deep, and quite long structure, and beyond it, on the far side, is what appears to be a market garden. Certainly a small-holding anyway. On our side, fallow fields lead to another wood, at the front edge of which is a river.

Once past the lock, the canal sweeps to the right, then straightens, for it's run into Swindon. However, before reaching that town, we have some modern homes to pass, each with gardens down to the edge of the water, a cricket ground, and reeds which give shelter to the moorhens and ducks along the far side. A solitary bench, offers rest at the edge of the towpath, worth a pause, if only to take in the peaceful scene.

A modern bridge Swindon No 40, crosses the waterway, and directly behind it, the towpath crosses the canal by means of a cast iron footbridge. Swindon lock is then next to the crossover point, and both sides of the water have houses with gardens down to the waterway. If you are in need of food, or refreshment, a few yards from the canal side is The Old Bush, which appears to be a popular meeting spot for locals.

The towpath is still of excellent walking surface, also wide and inviting, but the footway recrosses the water at the next lock, a mere hundred yards distant. Once more, it is preceded by a bridge, No 41, both bridge and lock being named Marsh. Grooves, made in the components of the bridge, by years of ropes attached to both horse and narrow boat, are clearly visible. Moorings have been available between the two locks, though the ones on the Western side, are private, and intended for the residents of the houses there.

After a mile or two of treeless banks, we enter the next section under the protective shade of the usual deciduous types, the other side also tree lined. As is now inevitable, our side sees the land fall below the water level, whilst it is raised above to the East. A lock cottage stands by the towpath, but is one with a difference. It has additional outbuildings, one with a stable door, complete with horseshoe over. We believe that this may be a point at which fresh horses were kept, in order to change and enable certain boats to continue with little pause. Whether or not this service would have been available to anyone, or if it were one particular company, has not been discovered on our walk.

We now reach Botterham, where bridge no 42 fronts a double lock. Both are quite deep. Beyond them is a 'plughole' overflow, once more typically Brindley. Near the top lock is another cottage, and in it's grounds are geese, and a small training field for horse riders. Our first moorhen of the day bustles noisily into the patch of reeds. Beyond the Hawthorn hedge to our left, a quality horse (hunter), complete with coat, looks out from roomy stables.

We follow the right hand curve, and can now see the roofs of Wombourne. There is also a large industrial estate to our left, though the right side consists of fields, down to the waters edge. A trio of geese, leave the far side, and, in anticipation of food, make their way slowly across. We have nothing for them, so they meander back to their vantage point. A large black and white building is ahead. Firstly it appears as if it will be to our left, but another curve in the canal, leaves it just off a main road, to our right. This is the Waggon and Horses, where meals are available at normal times. Now we pass under Wombourne Bridge, No 43, where some local anglers are intently watching floats. There are some moored boats along this section, private ones, and it is a very residential area with many properties close to the waterway. It looks a modern estate.

Bridge no 44, Giggety bridge, then immediately Giggety wharf, where two or three boats are being refitted. A mini marina by the looks of things. More properties with gardens down to the water, on the right, and a few yards further, some industrial buildings near to the path. Beyond them is a large industrial complex, by the appearance of the chimney, it's connected with the metal industry.

We have now reached Houndel Bridge, which consists of two actual structures. The original brick built one carries the road, whilst a recent metal one is for pedestrians. Close by, on the left, stands the Round Oak Public House. The original building has been extended, but without losing an olde world charm. Ample car parks, and a children's play area, complete the picture, and all is very inviting for food, drink, or both.

We still have modern housing, with sloping gardens on our right, many of them with moorings for their own craft.

Once more, the waterway curves to the right, and a steep path leads to bridge no 46, and its accompanying lock. The bridge merely goes to the garden of a spacious lock cottage, and is unusually steep. Even before we read the name, the scene is familiar from reading canal books. This is Bumblehole. I now know it's exact location, for the name and construction were all that I had read about. One of the lock gates is new, replaced as recently as 1997. More private boats are moored nearby, and the whole area of the canal, is a credit to the British Waterway staff, for it is beautifully restored.

A boat is about to enter the lock. It bears the name Porcillus, and comes from Devizes. Curiosity getting the better of me, I enquired what route they had followed, and how long they had travelled to reach this point. It transpired that the owners were about two thirds of the way through a six month cruise. Their craft looked as if it had just been completely painted, and was as neat and tidy as any seen on the waterways, so far.

A group of young lads are fishing nearby, well equipped, and equally well behaved, I hope they made good catches.

The canal widens, and we arrive at Bratch moorings. Just beyond are bridges 47 and 48, and a flight of three locks. Towering over all these, is the old Toll House, now used by the lock-keeper, Graham Durman as his office, and as a shop supplying memorabilia of the canal, and a range of most useful maps. Not only was Mr Durman helpful to all who passed through, but was most informative on technical, and other detail for which I asked.

To walk past the lower lock, there is a useful brick slope, but one notices the original stairway carved from rock. Beside two of the locks are pounds which supply water to maintain lock levels. More rope marks show above bridge 48, and we learn that until fairly recently, the Toll house was painted white.

The entire construction at Bratch locks, was reconstructed and modernised in 1994, but, as is the norm on this waterway, without spoiling the character, or destroying important historic features. Very close to Bratch stands a large Chateau styled building, complete with turrets. This is the local Headquarters of Severn Trent Water, who have provided a car park, and a picnic site for visitors.

A little way down the road from the locks, lies the former Wombourne Station, on the old Kingswinford Railway. This building has been converted into an excellent restaurant, and though primarily meant for walkers along the old track, it is well worth a visit by those walking the canal. I can vouch for the personal service, and the quality of Coffee and Tea.

There are seats by the side of the locks, and therefore one can enjoy a refreshment break, whilst watching Graham Durman or his deputy assist boaters through the complicated flight.

We have reached the end of the section, and it is only a short walk for West Midlands transport in Wombourne.

Botterham Staircase Lock

Section 5   Bratch to Compton 5 miles

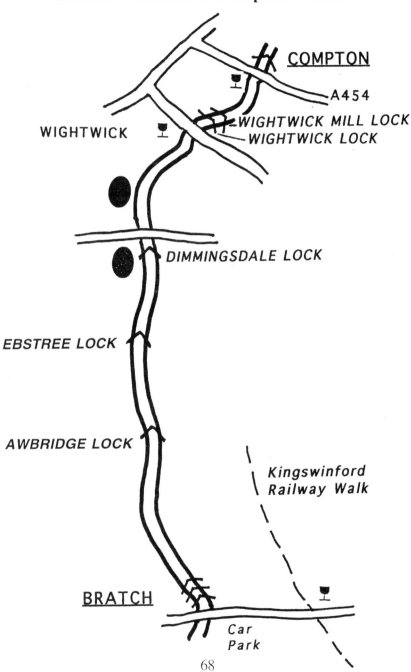

COMPTON

A454

WIGHTWICK MILL LOCK
WIGHTWICK LOCK

WIGHTWICK

DIMMINGSDALE LOCK

EBSTREE LOCK

AWBRIDGE LOCK

Kingswinford
Railway Walk

BRATCH

Car
Park

I was really looking forward to walking this next section of canal. Firstly, it included the earliest part of the waterway, secondly, I was curious to see whether or not, walking through a large conurbation, such as Wolverhampton, would be pleasant or otherwise. I need not have worried on the second count, for it was impossible to believe that the later part of the walk was within the boundary of a large city.

At Bratch, we crossed the water, and once more walked along the Eastern bank. just beyond the locks are moorings, with a number of boats, in varying condition, mostly privately owned.

Willows overhang the Left hand edges, and a Moorhen is seen gathering nesting materials, although it is already late July. However, it does appear that if conditions are good, these birds have more than one batch of young.

A cricket field is being mowed, and rolled, in preparation for a match, and the surroundings must be very relaxing for anyone who is connected with this club.

There is now a wide expanse of fields on both sides. To our right, they are bounded by a small wood. At this point, the canal is wide and clear, but as it swings to the right, the left bank is covered with a wide variety of vegetation.Now it straightens for some hundred yards, but at the next corner, turns to the left. Here, are bullrushes, just sufficient to allow shelter for a family of ducks. The panorama is mainly agricultural South Staffordshire.

A few reed beds narrow the water, and another turn to the right brings more delights.

Bridge no 49 at Awbridge looks as if it use be largely of original structure, and has an unusual design. At the centre part of each parapet, are columns of bricks, thus giving an opportunity to see through to the far side. Sunlight, passing through the spaces, makes it look, from a distance, as if the lock gate has holes in it. Common sense tells one that that is impossible, and closer examination proves it to be 'a trick of the light'. Between bridge and lock, is a cast iron footbridge for reaching the paddles, but it has no handrail and needs careful negotiation. A renovated lock cottage completes the group, and offers it's occupiers a clear view of passing boats.

Beyond the lock, and to the left, stands a farm, without evidence of occupation, but with a dominating Dutch barn. An overflow, of original Brindley design, is in full spate, following the upstream passage of two boats, and two other craft are moored under trees beyond the farm. The waterway curves left, then immediately right, into a long sweep.

Away to the left can be seen an Airship, though it is too far away to be identified. However, the boaters have seen it too, and point us in it's direction. A pipe crosses the water, in themanner of an additional bridge, and once again we curve to the left, at which point, the canal narrows considerably. There is evidence of brickworks here, which suggests a defunct bridge, but this is not on any map we have. The absence of number 51, suggests our surmise may be correct.

Two more turns, one in either direction, and we reach Ebstree bridge and lock. Here, we have a pleasant surprise, for the boat now passing through carries coal. This is the first freight carrying barge we have seen in our walk, so far, and is entitled 'Roach'. Crewed by a man and a woman, and lowering a metal chimney to pass beneath the bridge, we are told that, despite a reference to British Waterways, it is operating as an independent unit. Built in 1935, it was once operated by Fellows, Morton & Clayton, one of the largest freight boat fleets on our canals. It is beautifully decorated in traditional style, and is a tribute to waterway preservation.

A mere 'stones throw' along a short straight section, and we reach Dimmingsdale lock. Here, the towpath returns to the left side, where it remains for some distance. On this fine summer morning, the lock is busy, several boats waiting their turn to negotiate the obstacle. The coal carrier continues toward Wolverhampton.

This is a very pretty stretch, with trees lining both banks, and a large brown dragonfly skimming the water, as if to accompany our walk. As we reach an open section, a group of Canada Geese plop into the water, one by one, and check to see if food is available. They are unlucky, since the food was eaten at Dimmingsdale lock.

Several anglers are trying their luck, just before bridge no 53, also Dimmingsdale, and a small lake can be seen through a gap in the hawthorn hedge, it transpires that this is a private water, available only to members of a Black Country steel firm.

Just beyond the bridge, where Willow trees dominate the banks, there is a wall, and a disused wharf which, judging by the elaborate metal fencing, may well have once held a large stock of goods for transportation. The canal curves to the right, after which there is a very long straight section. Suddenly, away to the left, there is a second, and much larger lake.Probably man-made, certainly meant for fishing. The thick hedge makes it difficult to see the entire lake, but there are certainly quite a few anglers sitting along it's edges.

Beyond the tree-lined bank, on the far side, fields of crops wait to be harvested, and the water makes further turns in both directions. Swallows wheel over the surface collecting insects. What a skilled performance, for however low they fly, they always avoid contact with either the canal, or each other.

Mops farm bridge, no 54, crosses the waterway. Contrasting buildings are now passed, the older, presumably the farm itself, on our left, whilst a modernised structure, possibly several original cottages joined, is opposite. The light coloured walls dominate the far side. Baskets of flowers complete the decoration, and attract the eye.

Everywhere, the scene is rural and peaceful. A solitary Oak tree overhangs the towpath, and here and there, banks of thick-stemmed reeds can be seen. There are now Hawthorn hedges on either side. Though the width of the canal fluctuates, only under the bridges, it becomes too narrow for boats to pass each other. A Moorhen 'nods' it's merry way in and out of the vegetation to the right.

There have been numerous twists and turns in the waterway, but now, a long right hand sweep leads to the next bridge (no 55) at Castlecroft. The fields to the left are fallow, but signs of recent cultivation are apparent across the water. As we once more swing to the left, there are increasing signs of habitation. Some large houses, many with gardens down to the water's edge, dominate the far bank, and traffic can be heard on both sides, though the road away to the left is at the far end of a wide field.

Once more, the water sweeps to the right, and now there is another quite long straight section, along which are several moored boats. We can now see the road to the right, running parallel with the canal, and the increase in both traffic and properties, identify the fact that we are now on the outskirts of Wolverhampton. This is Wightwick (pronounced Wittik), and the bridge now crossing the water ahead of us carries a busy road from the city. Situated close to the waterway, just the other side of the Bridgnorth road, lies the Mermaid Inn. From the outside, it looks smart and interesting, whilst inside it is full of character and historical interest. At the appropriate time, there is a large range of food and drink available, and whether as a starting, mid-way or finishing point, it is well worth a visit.

One hundred yards up a hill, behind the Mermaid, lies Wightwick Manor. This was given to the National Trust by Sir Geoffrey Mander, a former local Member of Parliament, and whose name features much in the area. Constructed in the Victorian era, it is open to the public, though hours are limited, so one needs to check opening hours before arriving there.

We pass under Wightwick bridge (no 56), and very soon reach bridge 57, which fronts Wightwick lock. To the left of the lock stands one the usual cottages, right by the towpath, but although the garden is obviously well cared for, the building itself appears to be in a state of flux. However, it would be a pity to see this fall into disrepair, so we hope it is being re-furbished.

We now see a small craft entitled 'Midnight', complete with two people and a Labrador Dog. So typical of the many privately owned craft which are a credit to their owners.

A small stream flows beneath the canal, and it is only a short distance before we reach bridge no 58, and Wightwick Mill Lock. Two narrow boats from Anglo-Welsh accompany each other, as they pass between the two Wightwick locks. We notice friendly rivalry between them, as they operate the paddles and gates. The towpath is still in excellent condition, as it has been all the way from Kinver, and we again make favourable comments on the work carried out by British Waterways, to ensure that the canals remain operational, and the environs pleasant to use.

A 'plughole' overflow is operating whilst our companion boats pass through Mill lock, and the waterway is now in the full morning sun. Sparkling reflections cover the surface of the water, except where Ducks or Moorhens disturb the smoothness with their paddling. At this point, there is no sign of the modern metal edging, which shows that repair work has been needed. It appears that this may be original, but the banks are still in very good condition.

The canal has now re-commenced a meander, first to right, then to left, and in a now familiar pattern, the waterway has higher ground to the right, whilst the contour drops down to our left. This denotes consistency in construction, following the natural lie of the land. The water is wide, open, and clear, with only a few houses visible. Surely, we cannot really be within the boundaries of Wolverhampton!

A long right hand sweep, and a straight section, take us past an allotment, and several pleasantly converted buildings, into Compton. Here, the Bridge Restaurant looks worthy of a visit, and boaters are able to replenish supplies, water, and Diesel fuel. There is a Post Office and a Supermarket, and moorings are available within walking distance.

The bridge is no 59, and on the far side of it is a plaque which advises that in 1986, many of the surviving features from the original canal, were renovated. One presumes, therefore, that the waterway remained much the same as when first dug, for over two hundred years.

A few yards later we reach bridge no 60, which 'guards' the Compton lock. We are reminded that it was at this point that the first section of the Staffs/Worcs was dug, probably under the supervision of the great James Brindley himself. It is also recorded that Compton lock was the very first one built in the Midlands. The total cost of the whole canal £100,000.

Awbridge Lock

Compton

74

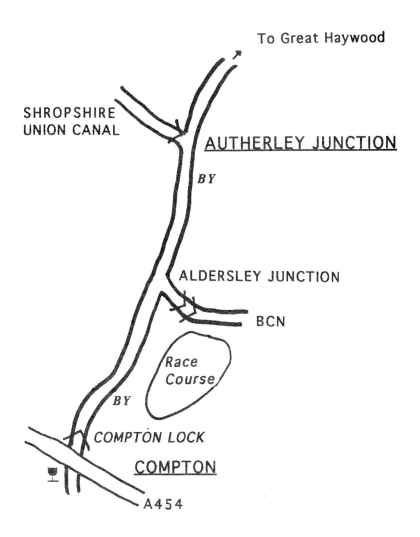

To Great Haywood

SHROPSHIRE
UNION CANAL

AUTHERLEY JUNCTION

BY

ALDERSLEY JUNCTION

BCN

Race
Course

BY

COMPTON LOCK

COMPTON

A454

I have to confess at my disappointment that apart from a plaque, there was little to show from the area, that linked with such a historical and momentous background. Anyone travelling through the section, without a guidebook, could easily be unaware of it's great significance We have already recorded that Brindley did not live long enough to see the completed project, even though it took a remarkably short time from 1765 to 1772. He was only 55 when he died, but in that fairly short life, he changed the face of Britain.

This is the highest point on the canal. All the way from Stourport, we had been rising with each lock, or flight, to a point nearly three hundred feet higher, but from now to Great Haywood, where it joins the Trent and Mersey Canal, it falls some one hundred feet. There are no more locks on the Staffs/Worcs, until after Autherley Junction, at which point our walking ends for this publication.

The ground to the right now slopes up into the woods, through long grassy areas, whilst the towpath edges onto other woodland. The canal continues as a wide open waterway, and we pass from shade to bright sunlight, and back again as the trees vary in height. Some boats are moored here for visiting Compton village.

Along this stretch are two long and deep overflows, which appear unnecessary, but on careful examination, one realises that the water is closer to the top of the bank, therefore they must be positioned as a precaution against flooding. There is a water depth guage, the first seen on either waterway.

The canal is now flanked on both sides by trees, leading along a very straight stretch toward the next bridge. Ducks and Moorhens are plentiful here, and it is interesting to note the wide variety of ages within the groups, evidence of several broods per year.

No longer are the trees mainly Willows and Oaks, as hitherto, but now there are Spruces, Birches, and Sycamore making up the woodlands. To the right, the ground widens out into a large outdoor sports complex which includes Football pitches and some well maintained grass Tennis courts.

The surface of the towpath has now reverted to it's original black substance, which means that mud patches can be anticipated in wet conditions, however in the height of Summer dryness, no problem. Now there are houses on both sides, some with gardens to the water's edge, and also several privately owned craft moored nearby.

We have reached Tettenhall, a well populated area, though still less crowded than I had originally expected. There are two bridges here, The Old no 61, and The New no 62. The old bridge carried the original coaching route between London and Holyhead, which included the Mail. However, an increase in traffic made it necessary to construct a larger new bridge. Fortunately, the old one remains for light local traffic, and access to the towpath from car parking and bus routes.. Close to the new bridge is Newbridge wharf, where there is a shop and other facilities for passing boats. A few yards further on another road bridge crosses the water, but also bears the number 62, a little confusing. Immediately, there is a former railway bridge, un-numbered, but in reasonably good condition.

We now see several boats moored on the far side, bearing the name Wolverhampton Passenger Boats. Their lay-out is obviously different from cruising craft. Near them is a modern, chalet style building, which is used for waiting passengers, and is also a nature centre. We are surprised to see more weeds in the water, than previously, but it does not affect the navigation. A short distance ahead, we see another bridge. It looks similar to most other older type bridges already seen, but we are in for something of a surprise. The first clue is the name, Tunstall Water Bridge, (no 63). We climb up to the top of the structure and find not only a footpath, but also a stream crossing the canal. In two separate ducts, of course.

The path leads toward a large open area where there are many gantries of floodlights, and we realise that this is Wolverhampton Race Course.

We return to the towpath, and a number of Ducks, of varying ages, drop into the water, on our approach. It is a bright morning, and the sun shines down from a clear blue sky. Reflections from the bridge clearly show it's features, and draw our attention to the repairs which have changed the brick colour in places. The path is strong again, and easily walked, the waterway is wide but peaceful, and there are many overhanging Willows on both sides. We commence a slow left hand curve, which leads to a very long straight section. We can now see a selection of bridges, crossing the canal at varying heights.

As we approach the first bridge, we notice that we have reached a junction. This is Aldersley, where the Birmingham Canal Navigations join the Staffs/Worcs by way of a lock. Opposite the junction stands a large signpost which offers the choice of Stourport, Birmingham, or Great Haywood. To join the towpath of the B C N, one must cross the bridge, no 64, near to which are seats for any budding 'Gongoozler'. Also, there is a site where, in days of horse-drawn boats, spare horses were stabled to be refreshed, and to await their next tour of duty.

There is a large turning area so that craft wishing to turn towards Stourport, have adequate room to manoeuvre, and moorings are in good supply.

We now get a good look at two very high bridges which look very well built. Just as well, for they carry the main railway line toward Telford.

These railway bridges, one in each direction, are high over the water, and their comparative newness means that they bear no bridge numbers. we can hear the trains, but not see them, unless one happens to be directly beneath when one passes. Three smaller and lower bridges, again un-numbered, follow in quick succession but their actual purpose is hard to decide. They are only wide enough for one small vehicle, and it would be difficult to understand, why three? if they are intended for pedestrians. Doubtless, the locals will know. A metal girder bridge carries pipes over the waterway, close to a large permanent mobile home park. This site is on the far side, but it looks as if they are quality homes, and quite sizable. From the number of units there, it might be a fairly recently established site.

The final bridge in this group, carries another busy main road, and is Oxley Moor, no 65.

The towpath rises steeply over a bridge, under which flows a stream. From the summit, we can see for the first time, our final destination, Autherley Junction. Moorings are now continuous right to the point where the Staffs/Worcs 'meets' the Shropshire Union Canal, on the far side being for privately owned craft/along the towpath are cruise boats, either resting, or waiting to turn onto the

'Shroppy'. The S and W continues toward Great Haywood, via another high bridge, but our path passes under this structure to reveal the shallow rise lock onto the new waterway.

Aldersley Junction

Part Three

The Stourbridge Canal
(including the Stourbridge Town Arm)

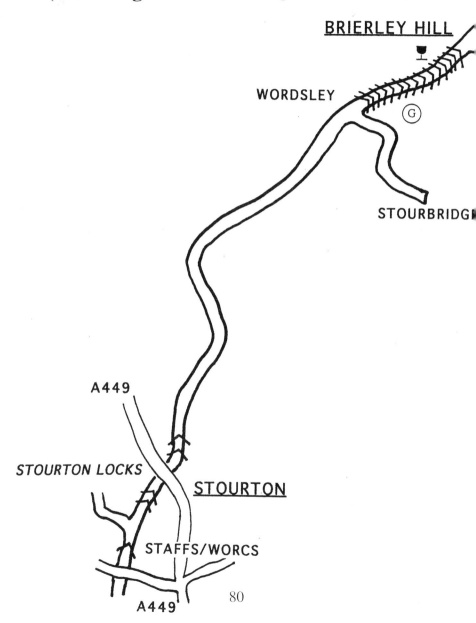

BRIERLEY HILL

WORDSLEY

(G)

STOURBRIDGE

A449

STOURTON LOCKS

STOURTON

STAFFS/WORCS

A449

80

The Stourbridge Canal walk commences at the junction of the Staffs/ Worcs at Stourton, but for a shorter walk it is also possible to omit the early part and start at Wordsley.

This canal is worthy of, nay it demands, a separate narrative, from the main series of walks, and from it's differing characteristics, is really two canals in one. On the day that this waterway was on the agenda, for walking, it seemed that there were many people who agreed with the sentiment expressed in Kenneth Grahame's masterpiece 'The Wind in the Willows', in which he stated that " There is nothing so good as messing about in Boats". More boats than was usual were encountered all along this fascinating canal as it was in the height of the cruising season.

Joining the towpath at Stewpony Lock, Stourton, there was much history to be learned. Firstly a collection of buildings, standing at the site of a former busy wharf, included a Toll house, dating from 1772. Early photographs show that this was a significant centre for freight. Now, the old Toll house is a shop, but one with a difference. Apart from the usual sweets, ice-cream and mementos, the owner dispenses 'Clairvoyance'. He is a noted Psychic, who is heavily into Ghost hunting, but with particular emphasis on the districts of Stourton and Kinver. It is said that the last Highwayman to be hanged in this country, ended his days on the nearby gibbet.

We were greeted cheerily, by a couple just leaving Stewpony Lock, typical of most cruising people, who were heading toward Wolverhampton. Moored craft were only gently rocked by their considerate speed, and their engine was extremely quiet. Private boats are moored on the far side, at this point.

We left the main canal via Stourton bridge near to a clear signpost, and walked toward the first of four locks and taking us under the main A449 trunk road. The first two locks are separated by a short length of water, from which a private mooring leads to large gardens. After the second lock. we pass through a tunnel, and find it necessary to cross over the water, by means of a metal footbridge. This was one of those where a split divided the bridge, so allowing Horses to pass without being unhitched from their towed craft. All part of canal History.

At this point, a modernised lock cottage stands on the side we have just left, and there is a third lock. The towpath has been made firm with modern materials, and remains that way throughout the entire length of our walk.

We are now passing a group of quality homes, each with garden running to the waters edge, but fields stretch away from the towpath as far as the eye can see.

We reach the fourth lock, and with growing excitement note a freight boat awaiting descent. I discover that this is no ordinary boat, and that it featured prominently in the campaign to return the waterways to leisure use. Named the 'Hesperus', though that was not it's original name, it was built at Rickmansworth on the Grand Union Canal, in 1935. It once belonged to Lord Lucan (wherever he may now be) when he was Chairman of the Inland Waterways Association, and was used at rallies to help promote the use of waterways.

No sooner had Hesperus passed through the lock, there was another, smaller freight boat about to enter. This was 'Chipp No 4', being operated by the New City Canal Transport Company, and it had left Stourbridge terminus an hour previously. Whilst waiting for the lock to refill, the crew treated us to a potted version of canal transport. Some narrow boats used to run all the way along various canals, from Stourport to Liverpool, whilst others were engaged in local round trips, often two or three in a day. These were specially constructed so that the steering tillers could be changed to either end of a boat, thus enabling it to avoid having to turn around, in what were often limited spaces. Skippers often owned their own Tillers, which could be moved from one boat to another, and which were often highly decorated.

In a short space of time, we had learned something about canal history.

As the houses are left behind, willows overhang the water, on the far side, and water lilies of the more unusual yellow colour, top the surface of the water. Moorhens fly from the path, into the murky waters, and there are now joggers and Dog walkers joining us on the towpath. The canal is just wide enough for boats to pass, but in places, widens further, only to narrow as bridges are neared. In the distance, woodlands can be seen, together with isolated farms, and the clubhouse of the Stourbridge Rugby Union Football Club. There are some reeds on the opposite side, which temporarily restrict two-boat navigation, and a small private wood, next to the towpath, has been fenced off, with metal palings.

Oaks and Alders spread their branches over our walkway, and in places the original timber linings of the canal bank, can be identified. In Summer, Swallows fly across the surface of the water, collecting insects, and during the same season, Dragonflies and various water creatures complete the scene.

We round a new corner to see a bridge, beyond which there is a small boatbuilders, and several moored boats. Boats under construction appear to be metal hulled, and there is some welding in progress.

Another turn in the waterway, and the width increases, the extra surface increasing the reflections from a bright sky, and where the trees are less dense. Another farm bridge is sited on yet another turn, and a large bird rises from the bank, and flies low beyond the water, and toward shelter at the edge of a field. Yes, a Heron. I had not seen him, but his keen eye watched our approach, which demonstrates the importance of comparative silence, should one wish to see all the wildlife in the area. I suspect that these birds are highly territorial, and that there will be a chance that we might see him on our return.

Through trees, at the edge of the path, we can see a small river. In fact, we could hear it rushing over a waterfall, before it came into view. Although this canal was built long after James Brindley designed the Staffs/Worcs, the same principal of using natural contours, and river valleys as the line of the canal, seems to have been used. Both waters run parallel for some distance, whilst on the further side, fields reach down to the water's edge, and there are a number of Horses grazing nearby. A Squirrel darts up a tree, close by, and a family of Ducks make a 'V' shaped ripple as they pass along. There is now another footbridge, used by local inhabitants to pass from nearby housing, toward shops in Wordsley, also it is popular with those walking their dogs.

A pair of Swans, the first seen that day, cavort and dip in the water, also preening and 'tipping up' to find tempting morsels of vegetation beneath the surface. More Ducks occupy a mass of dried reed, and there is a possibility that this may have been a nesting site for the Swans, although no Cygnets are in evidence.

Narrowing to pass over a bridge and stream, the canal nears the next Junction, from where another walk, this time to the Stourbridge terminus, can be taken. The wide turning area allows for whatever direction boaters wish to travel, and there is a low wall close to mooring bolts which provides a seat for rest and refreshment, prior to tackling sixteen locks, in an uphill direction.

To our left, we can see the tower of Holy Trinity Church, Wordsley, and a well populated area. There is a boat descending through the first lock no 16, since they are numbered from the top of the flight. Fresh molehills of very dark soil, stand proud of the green grass at the rim of the lock brickwork, but their options are limited, unless they can swim.

Almost immediately, there is a second lock, complete with winding hole, and just beyond a road bridge, a third. There is some industry nearby, but the immediate surroundings of the canal are still mainly residential, though the houses to the left are well below the level of the waterway, whilst those on the far side, are above. Each lock has a sloping path beside it, the steepness varying according to the lock depth. Steps are also provided for the convenience of those crew members who are delegated to work the paddles.

There is a longer stretch of water, prior to reaching the fourth lock, at which point the main Stourbridge to Brierley Hill road crosses by way of 'Glasshouse Bridge. This is so named because at this place, the Internationally known firm of Glassmakers, Stuart Crystal has it's factory. There is a museum, a shop, and a public restaurant at Stuarts, and for the convenience of canal users, a mooring for their boats.

The towpath is fully tarmacked, and there is a glass case by the waterway which displays information on the history, and funding of the Stourbridge Canal. An Act of Parliament was passed in 1776, authorising the building of this waterway. It was completed in 1779, at a cost of £38,000, which by most standards, was a rapid feat.

The project was funded by Viscount Dudley and Ward, Earl of Stamford, and for many years, industry was indebted to this philanthropist, as we users are today.

84

Within a short walking distance of the waterway, another renowned Midland company, Webbs, the seed and garden 'merchants have their offices.

A few yards further along the towpath, and on the far side can be seen a notice 'The Vine, Banks's Beers'. We feel that it must be a Public House, but the building is all wrong. It is a modern pre-fabricated construction, which suggests it may be a works club. It is the name which does not fit that theory.

We pass under yet another bridge, and the fifth lock comes into view. This bears the number twelve, which, until we realised that the builders were counting downwards made little sense.

Above this lock, several boats are moored, alongside a ware-house. It would appear to be connected with British Waterways, and is possibly a depot.

Three more locks follow in quick succession, and there is a narrow footbridge, just before the last of these. There is also a double lock cottage nearby, adding atmosphere.

Many boats were seen during that walk, especially negotiating the various locks, but the ones which caused most interest, were those being crewed by overseas visitors. Noticing one from Alvechurch, 'a totally different canal start, we enquired their route. It transpired that they had negotiated a large section of the Birmingham system to reach this spot. All they wanted to know was "How many more Locks are there?". I am not certain that they appreciated my reply.

Not many Anglers along this stretch, but there were British Waterways workers repairing a section of brickwork. As usual, they were not only polite, but also interesting to talk to.

Two more locks, a bridge between them, and a colourless piece of towpath, except for a bright pink Lavatera in full bloom. Another three locks, and we reached the 'Samson and Lion' Pub, though, despite it being close to mid-day, no apparent activity there. Hope the boat crews were not unduly hungry or thirsty. There was, however, a notice advertising Sunday Lunches, so perhaps anyone travelling on a Sunday would find the place bustling with action.

Our way takes us under another main road, and memory of the road system suggests we were close to Brierley Hill.

The canal is now wide, with a high standard of maintenance. There are now only three more locks to the top of the flight, and the end of a fairly long walk, especially when we remembered, that we had to go all the way to Stourton, to pick up the car.

On the final stretch, there were some factories, but houses still formed the majority of buildings, the most significant contribution to a rural atmosphere being the notice, close to the towpath which stated "Dudley Wildlife Area".

Redhouse Glassworks

Stourbridge Branch Canal
Wordsley junction to Stourbridge terminus.

Before I commenced writing about this small section of canal, I read that it should not really be titled a "branch", since it's construction preceded that of the Wordsley - Brierley Hill, sixteen lock section. I also note in the 'Canals and Waterways' monthly publication, (a must for all canal users), there is a campaign to have this section updated in status. This is due to the large volume of tourist traffic. After reading this walk, you may agree with me, that some considerable work is needed, if the suggestion can be taken seriously.

Dependent on where one commences the walk. Stourton, Wordsley, or any point between, this canal provides a totally different aspect to any other yet encountered. It is very similar to the most industrial areas of Kidderminster, surrounded by commercial units, and somewhat neglected. However, it should not be missed out for those reasons, for all canals are worthy of investigation and walking, if only as a comparison, and as a real insight into original use. The towpath is original, so requires heavier footwear, and some measure of sure-footedness. There is mud, there have been no attempts to improve the surface for serious walkers.

The first bridge, is aptly titled 'Longboat Lane Bridge', and the presence of trees, a high banking, and buildings give a dark, almost forbidding aura. There are some early cottages, numbered? The Junction, one of which has the inscription "Built 1829 by Guest" In between two lots of cottages, a modern Bungalow has been built, which, though nice, seems a little out of place. Under another bridge, apparently untouched since the construction of this canal, we see, across the water, what appear to be derelict warehouses. Despite the broken windows, and worn fabric of these, I notice lights in these buildings, together with the sound of machinery. I cannot help but wonder how they manage in bad weather!

Near to the path, there are new housing estates, and on the far side, several boats are moored. These seem to be under renovation.

Another bridge, carrying a road, and the canal is very narrow, with reeds, and other vegetation, making navigation a little difficult. The towpath is also at it's muddiest, yet right in the midst, I see a young man walking toward me, dressed in business suit, with shoes polished for the town, and carrying a rolled umbrella and briefcase. Is he taking a short cut? Well, he certainly was not dressed for walking along that section.

The water widens, but is still thick with vegetation, including water lilies showing yellow flowers, and trying to catch the sun. A dried-up overflow, leading to a choked stream leaves the waterway, but even with passing boats, does not seem to have carried water for some time. The path now rises over three high bridges, leading at some past time over industrial inlets, where goods could have been loaded inside factory premises, ready for transport to other areas.

Some of the factories remain operational, whilst others are quite derelict, abandoned heaps of metal marking the once busy sites.

At the end of the section, which has been merely a mile in length, a large number of narrow boats are moored, many of them florally decorated. There is a Bonded Warehouse, and from here, walkers are denied further access. All one can do, is to retrace ones steps, back to the Junction.

There is a feeling of success and triumph, now that our project is complete, but also a tinge of sadness in leaving the Midlands Canals for the time being.

Springtime by the Canal

COMMON VETCH

COLTSFOOT

INDEX

C cont.

D

E

F

G

H

H cont.

I

J

K

L

M

N

O

P

Q

R

S

S cont.

T

V

W

Maps are not to scale, but approx 1 $^1/2$" to 1 mile as general guide.

SIGNS AND SYMBOLS

CANAL

TUNNEL WITH NO TOWPATH

A449 ROADS (ALL CLASSES)

RAILWAYS
RAILWAYS DISUSED

RESERVOIR OR AREA
OF WATER

AREA OF BEAUTY / PARK

BY BOAT YARD

PUB / HOTEL REFRESHMENT

LOCK - UPWARDS DIRECTION

LOCK - DOWNWARDS DIRECTION

(G) GLASSWORKS

CIVIL WAR CENTRE

WINDMILL